Horror Trope Thesaurus

Killing It With Tropes

Jennifer Hilt

For horror fans, the horror curious, and anyone who writes tortured characters.

Contents

Part Two

Part Three

Welcome to the Horror Trope Thesaurus

I'm back for more trope talk. And honestly, I'm pretty stinking excited about it. In *The Trope Thesaurus* I didn't include the horror genre because I had a suspicion there was a lot there to dig into.

Little did I know when I started researching horror it would send me down a most delicious rabbit hole. This has been my favorite book to write and that is a wonderful feeling to savor. If I didn't at least try to keep my deadlines, I could be adding to this for a very long time.

In *The Trope Thesaurus,* I talk about tropes as storytelling building blocks. It's our job to shape them into specific molds to fit our stories. One way to do that is using Goal, Motivation, and Conflict with tropes to build our story.

I believe GMC and tropes go hand and hand but there's so much to talk about with horror, we're not going to rehash *The Trope Thesaurus* ideas here.

When I wrote *The Trope Thesaurus,* I had no idea if anyone would find my observations helpful. I'm grateful that it has provided encouragement to some writers because this is a lonely business. And really, we don't need life to be any more challenging than it already is. No matter what genres we write in, my hope is that *Horror Trope Thesaurus* will encourage us as storytellers to create our best monsters.

The Horror Genre and Tropes

Take It Personally

Remember in *The Sixth Sense* (1999), the traumatized child tells psychologist Bruce Willis, "I see dead people"?

Yeah, well I see tropes everywhere.

Sometimes they are easier to spot than others, but the closer I look I know they are there. I'm firmly in camp #teamtrope which is how *The Trope Thesaurus* came to be. Finally, all my reading and binge viewing across romance, mystery, fantasy, and science fiction made sense. I didn't need a specific genre. I needed a great story.

But I never suspected I was a horror fan.

Sure, the signs were there. I have a pretty high tolerance for zombies. I'm in awe of Jordan Peele movies. And I have a thing for the creepiness of the Bronte sisters, Shirley Jackson, and Edgar Allen Poe stories. Plus, don't get me started on the early seasons of *Penny Dreadful.*

The thrill those stories gave me felt like a dirty little secret. I realized when I entered a physical bookstore, I always scouted for the horror section. Granted, they are pretty hard to find these days but when I did, it was bliss being among the monsters. These were my people.

Ok but liking some literary horror was a far cry from being a slasher fan, right? Was I going to be fangirling over *Gingerbread Man 3: Saturday Night Cleaver* (2011)? Perhaps I'd taken this trope thing a bit too far.

So, I ventured forth into my deep dive into a variety of subgenres in horror movies and series. I did not consume any horror sequels. It's much easier to discuss visual storytelling because it's easily available to us all now.

I never knew how hardcore a horror fan I was until this book poured out of me. I'd find myself discussing the story structure of *Saw* over family dinner exclaiming, "It's all relationships and forced proximity!" Though, in retrospect my audience didn't appear surprised at my fork-waving proclamations.

For someone who lives and breathes tracking tropes, you'd think I'd have figured out that the horror genre is packed with tropes. I mean, I suspected as much to take on this project.

But I was shocked to realize that tropes were so integral to the horror genre.

Horror is the genre that always surprises me. It's where I learned, "Hey, I didn't know you could do *that*."

And that's because the Horror genre is so rich in tropes and how to twist them. I love the creativity in horror.

Whether you write Horror or not or are a fan, it's just fun seeing how the pieces all work together.

The Trope Thesaurus (TT) is all about my belief that tropes are essential story building blocks. TT goes into detail about my thoughts on using this potential storytelling superpower.

I'm not a fan of repetition and I'm eager to get on with discussing horror and tropes so I'll just give a brief recap here.

A trope is a commonly held idea that doesn't need much (if any) explanation. A few trope examples are **best friends**, **forced proximity**, and **victim**. You know what I'm talking about without me having to go into any definitions.

A trope is a neutral building block. It's a raw material that can be molded into what your story needs.

For me, stereotypes/clichés are not the same as tropes because the former is a fixed idea with a value judgment.

For example, the stereotype/cliché dumb jock describes a negative fixed idea. It's demeaning. It shuts down character development.

However, if you want to create a character who is an athlete that gives you the freedom to develop any qualities you want for that person.

My rule of thumb for wondering if something is a stereotype/cliché is: would I use it to describe someone I value in my life? If not, then discard it.

We are in the story creation business. Our characters need to live and breathe. They must have all the complexity of those we meet in real life.

Not surprisingly, I'm not interested in stereotypes/clichés because all the storytelling action is in twisting tropes.

Now that we know a trope is a story building block, let's get down to defining horror.

I researched many definitions of horror. It's amazing and impressive how diverse the genre is. But horror boils down to one key element: monsters.

Let's define the horror genre as the study of our relationships with monsters.

The important pieces in the sentence above are: relationships and monsters.

Now we get to the best part, what is a monster? And why do we care?

A monster can be a zombie, an alien, or even us. Its form can be anything. But the key is that whatever form the monster takes has to tap into the protagonist's deepest relationship fear—their dread. This is critical to remember.

The monster can be a character's boyfriend (*Scream*), their child (*The Omen),* the friendly community canine (*Cujo*) or even our memories (*Get Out*).

Before researching this book, I shied away from visual storytelling because I feared random mindless violence. Heck, I'm busy enough avoiding the news, there's no way I'm voluntarily taking that journey.

My discovery consuming these thirty-plus movies and series was that the horror genre was **not** random violence. (Again, I can't speak to horror movie sequels).

Horror is about dread in relationships.

The more vulnerable our protagonists are to the monster, the greater the challenges they have to overcome. And that has the makings of a great story.

And that was a shocker for me in writing this book.

The horror genre is about relationships. And the more personal, the better the story.

And guess what? So are tropes. That's why audiences react instinctively to them.

The question isn't, "should I use tropes or not?" You're already using them. Shouldn't you be using them to their greatest impact?

You do this by using tropes to build relationships that capture characters who ensnare readers. And by avoiding generic descriptions.

Remember the popular writing maxim: *complex characters, simple plot*?

That's still our goal.

We create complex characters but giving them desires that will shake them to the core of their being. We give them layers and conflicting impulses. Afterall, we're all complicated individuals, we should give our characters the same opportunity.

We're going to see how tropes are everywhere in horror and how they link together to form relationships.

Honestly, I'm so stinking excited to talk about horror with you, I'm giddy. Let's do this!

We want to see characters who are like us, conflicted, messy, uncertain, etc. BUT with clear, simple, GOALS.

Simple Goals, conflicted characters.

I wonder if these tropes will be useful – actually identifiable, but I think it will be great building blocks for my own stories.

How This Book Works

Ok, it's easiest if I use examples that are readily available via streaming services so that's where you can find any of these movies and series.

In **Part I**, we'll look at thirty-plus tropes commonly found in the horror genre. I created a trope synopsis for each highlighting the all the various tropes in that example. You're going to see a lot of tropes and a lot of overlap. This is a good thing! I want you to see that in addition to tropes being everywhere, they can be combined in an infinite number of ways.

In **Part II**, we'll study twelve key horror tropes by using comparison examples of movies/series of the first thirty movies we just talked about. These are the tropes that we find in pretty much every story. For example, we can see how the **forced proximity trope** is used in different ways with other tropes to build relationships.

In **Part III**, we'll have an **All-Amnesia trope** love fest. Whether you love or hate the amnesia trope or perhaps don't know how to use it, come celebrate some innovative uses of this trope. It plays so very well with others.

It's fun to see all these tropes in storytelling plus I hope it inspires you to tackle your own projects with new enthusiasm.

So, here's the game plan Horror peeps:

1. I'm going to show you common tropes are used in the horror genre.
2. We'll discuss the why and how they are used and why you should be using them.
3. And lastly, I'll show you useful ways tropes work together to describe relationships.

Ready to peel back the curtain and look at the inner workings of the horror genre?

Part One

In the following examples, if I run across a trope in the story, I'm going to highlight it even if we don't go into detail in this book on it. For example, the **opposites attract** and **mentor tropes**, are not super common in horror but it pops up here and there, so I point it out when I see it.

Also, I don't go into secondary characters unless they are important to the story. If they were just a **victim**, I'm leaving it at that. But in your own work please develop those characters because the quirky side characters can be story telling gold.

In mystery writing circles, there's a famous piece of advice—don't introduce a gun in the first act that won't go off in the third.

Guess what? That applies to tropes! We don't want to introduce a trope then fail to develop it.

Think of tropes as threads; loose ends aren't your enemies here, not if you can give it a tug and more of the protagonist's life unravels. That creates more story conflict, which we love.

Now here's an example of an underdeveloped trope in *World War Z*. The protagonist Gerry's GMC is his family's safety—that's a HUGE relationship issue. That is how the story is set up, I'm primed and ready for a big **family** safety showdown.

But is that what's threatened in the climax? Nope.

Is that a big story problem? Yep.

Don't leave a trope thread hanging. It's a problem not even Brad Pitt can solve.

*Incidentally, how I'd fix it is having one of his daughters bitten by a zombie. How would *you* fix it?

Writing out the tropes synopsis reminds me of the "show your work" mantra in math. When it's all laid out, seeing where it does or doesn't add up at the end is easier.

Now it's time to check out some trope descriptions.

Across the Tracks/Wrong Side of the Tracks

Silence of the Lambs (1991)

The **across the tracks trope** (ATT) refers to the unequal relationship between two parties, frequently employed to highlight one character's wealth versus the other's lack of resources. But **ATT** can create more conflict than just finances. Take a look at our example below.

Trope Synopsis *Silence of the Lambs*:

Clarice Starling, aspiring FBI agent (**loner**, **orphan**, **profession**, **scar**) interviews (**fish out of water**) famous serial killer Hannibal Lecter (**antagonist**, **billionaire**, **suspect**) in his prison (**forced proximity**, **workplace**) hoping to gain insight (**quest**) into an evasive serial killer (**MacGuffin**). He's bored with prison, so he offers to help track down the killer (**mentor**) in exchange for information (**the bet/wager**) about her early **tortured-heroine** life (**fairy tale**, **secrets**).

When another inmate insults Claire during her visit, Lecter (**protector**, **suspect**) convinces him to kill himself (**victim**, **violence**). Lecter's physician, Dr. Chilton (**antagonist**, **boss**, **profession**) sees Hannibal as a way to make a name for himself in the psychiatry field (**fake relationship**). Clarice is trying to find (**MacGuffin**, **quest**) Buffalo Bill (**antagonist**, **hidden identity**, **MacGuffin**, **suspect**, **violence**), the suspected serial killer of several women.

Lecter and Clarice share (**across the tracks**, **age difference**, **mentor**, **opposites attract**) a relationship with mutual fascination. Clarice suffers from **amnesia** about her childhood trauma but eventually, she reveals her worst childhood memory (**return to hometown**, **scar**).

Meanwhile, she's searching for Buffalo Bill's latest **victim** (**kidnapped**, **politics**, **stranded**, **ticking time bomb**, **violence**, **women in peril**).

Lecter escapes prison (**road trip**, **suspect**), gruesomely killing his guards (**victims**, **violence**) while Clarice **stalks** Buffalo Bill's **hidden identity**. Eventually, she locates the killer with what she's learned from Lecter (**mentor**), kills Buffalo Bill, and saves the senator's daughter (**redemption**).

Lecter calls her (**reunion**) from his travels abroad with Dr. Chilton.

How the **across the tracks trope** is used in *Silence of the Lambs*: Lecter is cultured and educated as opposed to Clarice's inexperience and more humble upbringing.

That unequal gap between them raises the story tension because even though Hannibal is behind bars, he's still able to hurt Clarice emotionally. Here's my favorite line of the movie that sums this trope up, Hannibal says, "You come in here with your cheap shoes and expensive handbag..." He's pierced the carefully constructed image she has of herself as a professional woman.

Best Friend

Cujo (1983)

We all know who's man's **best friend**, right?

Trope Synopsis *Cujo*:

A beloved dog, Cujo (**antagonist**, **best friend**) is bitten by a rabid bat (**hidden identity**) which causes him to become **violent** without any warning (**secret**). Two men are Cujo's (**suspect**) first **victims**; his neighbor and the father of his young owner.

While these dead bodies are cooling on the property, Donna and her young son, Tad (**family**), drive out to Cujo's family farm for some car repairs. They are shocked when Cujo attacks them (**ticking time bomb**, **violence**), **stranding** them in their now non-functional car with no means of escape as the summer day heats (**forced proximity**).

Donna's husband returns home from out of town (**return to hometown**). His house has been vandalized by Donna's current lover (**fake relationship**, **love triangle**, **secrets**). When he discovers his wife and son are missing, he fears her lover might have harmed them and alerts the sheriff (**red herring**). The sheriff arrests the wife's lover, but he pleads innocent. Instead, Donna's husband remembers she was taking the car to get it worked on.

The sheriff (**protector**) comes out to investigate, discovering the corpses. But Cujo (**suspect**) kills him (**victim**) before he can alert help.

Cujo attacks the car every time she tries to start it, but eventually Donna (**woman in peril**) decides she has no choice. She and her son could die of heat stroke if she doesn't get help. She slips out of the car but Cujo attacks, biting her leg (**victim**). She returns to the relative safety of the car (**forced proximity**, **stranded**) where she spies a bat outside the car (**quest**). She tries again to leave the car and reach the bat (**second chance**). This time when Cujo attacks, she beats him back before finally impaling him with a broken bat's wooden stake (**suspect**, **victim**, **violence**). She thinks he's dead (**red herring**). But Cujo isn't dead; he attacks again (**the con**). This time she grabs the dead sheriff's discarded gun and kills Cujo (**revenge**, **redemption**). The **family** is **reunited**.

How the **best friend trope** is used in *Cujo*: horror legend Stephen King twisting the **best friend trope** into a canine **antagonist**? Simple, yet elegant. King used our familiarity with dogs as benevolent to surprise us with a story about a vicious killer. Random fact I read while researching this movie: The Saint Bernard breed used in the movie was so friendly they had to either tie the dogs' tails down or not show their wildly wagging tails in any scenes.

I like reading the Synopses
but idk

Bet/Wager

Saw (2004)

The **bet/wager trope** describes a relationship question where the outcome is not guaranteed, and a certain amount of risk is at stake. If the bet/wager fails, things shouldn't just return to the normal state with no consequences.

Trope Synopsis *Saw*:

The story begins with two men waking to find themselves in a horrifying, but fairly novel situation. Adam and Dr. Gordon (**amnesia**, **forced proximity**, **kidnapped**, **profession**) is chained up and locked in a room with a corpse (**victim**) and some saws. Soon, they discover the reason that they are there; to save his (**family**), Dr. Gordon (**fish out of water**, **suspect**) must kill Adam (**fish out of water**, **victim**) by six pm to save his wife (**family**, **ticking time bomb**). This is another game (**bet/wager**) created by an elusive serial killer, Jigsaw (**antagonist**, **hidden identity**).

Previously, Dr. Gordon was a Jigsaw **suspect** (**mistaken identity**, **red herring**) which interrupted his work as an oncologist (**profession**). After being cleared of suspicion, detectives Tapp and Sing (**best friend**, **politics**, **professions**, **protector**) involved Gordon in the investigation (**quest**) interviewing the only surviving Jigsaw **victim**.

Still, in the past, we see Tapp and Sing find Jigsaw's hideout (**MacGuffin**) and they free his latest **victim**. Jigsaw escapes but not before killing Sing (**victim**) with his booby traps. Afterward, a grieving Tapp **stalks** Gordon, still believing he is Jigsaw (**red herring**).

Meanwhile, Jigsaw's other victims, Gordon's family, can see him through a camera. His wife calls him, telling him not to trust Adam (**fake relationship**). Adam reveals he was **stalking** Gordon for Tapp. Adam shows Gordon pictures of him entering a motel with one of his medical students (**love triangle**, **red herring**). Gordon concludes that he is being punished for adultery when he did not have an affair (**fake relationship**). In the pictures, Gordon recognizes Zap, an orderly at his hospital (**profession**, **workplace**), and suspects (**red herring**) him of being Jigsaw.

Zap has **kidnapped** Gordon's family. When the time is up at six pm (**ticking time bomb**), Zap goes to kill Gordon's wife (**woman in peril**), but she fights back (**violence**). Now, Gordon hears screams but has no idea what's going on with his family (**tortured hero**).

Gordon shoots Adam and then uses the saw to cut off his chained foot (**scar**).

Zap arrives at the bathroom, stalked by Tapp, and shoots him (**violence**). Zap tells Gordon the game is up (**bet/wager**). The wounded Adam kills Zap. Gordon crawls away (**second chance**), promising to get help.

Tortured hero Adam finds a tape on Zap which reveals he was playing a game too (**bet/wager**) he was not Jigsaw (**mistaken identity**).

The corpse on the floor isn't dead (**hidden identity**) to Adam's shock. It's Jigsaw (**antagonist**) who also happens to be one of Dr. Gordon's terminal brain cancer patients, John (**hidden identity**, **loner**, **revenge**, **scars**, **secrets**, **stalker**, **ugly duckling**).

Jigsaw/John tells Adam the key to his shackle washed down the drain earlier (**MacGuffin**). Jigsaw reveals his games (**bet/wager**) are intended to make people appreciate life (**second chance**), but Adam has lost the game (**victim**). Jigsaw leaves him sealed in the bathroom to die.

How the bet/wager trope is used in *Saw*: The **bet/wager tropes** drive the conflict for this entire story because the main characters play at least two roles if not more to increase the story tension. Also, it reminds me of two other things: (1) The legend of a wolf chewing off its foot to survive when caught in a trap and (2) Grimm's *Hansel and Gretel*.

BLACKMAIL

KINGDOM (2019) NETFLIX

Blackmail is a means of motivating another character's behavior by threatening someone with divulging their **secret**.

TROPE SYNOPSIS *KINGDOM*:

The main *Kingdom* plot involves a struggle for the Korean throne (**politics**, **quest**) between a reluctant **illegitimate** (**across the tracks**, **tortured hero**) **prince** against a rival clan faction led by the queen and her father (**antagonists**), the chief councilor.

Our story opens with the **royalty trope** as the Korean king is sick, possibly close to death. No one except the cunning chief councilor (**boss**, **military**) and his daughter, the queen (**arranged marriage**, **family**) knows the King's health status (**secret**). They **con** everyone into believing he is gravely ill when they have made him into a zombie (**antagonist**). The queen has falsified her pregnancy (**con**) because for her to retain power, she must deliver a son. Her **secret** is known only to a few trusted **domestic servants**. Meanwhile, beyond the palace walls, famine and murmurs of a strange illness are sweeping the impoverished countryside villages (**across the tracks**, **victims**).

The crown prince, Chang, has two loyal supporters. One is his long-time trusted servant (**best friend**, **protector**, **age gap**) Moo-young. The other is a Seo-bi, a young doctor (**loner**, **profession**, **protector**), who battles furiously to find the cause (**MacGuffin**) of the zombie outbreak.

With the queen's impending delivery (**ticking time bomb**), the crown prince is determined to discover what ails his father by going in search of the physician treating him (**road trip**, **fish out of water**) against the queen's wishes. As a result, he has been labeled a traitor and the queen's army (**military**) searches for him. But the crown prince assumes a **hidden identity** as he makes his way to the physician's compound with his loyal bodyguard.

The next day, the prince and bodyguard arrive to discover the compound deserted but having recently hosted a bloody battle with many dead bodies (**victims**).

Seo-bi and the warrior return to the compound along with the queen's army **stalking** the prince all just as night falls (**ticking time bomb**). The zombies awaken and a fierce battle begins in the compound (**forced proximity**).

The prince killed the chief councilor's beloved son. This sent the powerful warlord into an elaborate **revenge** plan: Chang was locked in a room (**forced proximity**, **scar**) with his zombie father. He killed him rather than be turned into a zombie himself (**tortured hero**).

Another **revenge** plot was enacted by the mysterious warrior who helps Seo-bi and the prince. The warrior's village was wiped out three years ago and then turned into zombies to fight the impending Japanese invasion; the plan was created by the chief councilor and another lord.

The prince's group assumes the zombies are impacted by sunlight not understanding it is about temperature (**red herring**). They are **stranded**, surrounded by zombies.

The relationship that the lonely prince values the most is between him and his bodyguard. That's why when the queen's representative **blackmails** the bodyguard, that betrayal cripples the prince.

Relationships between the doctor, the prince, and the Magistrate (**love triangle**) ensue. The magistrate (**boss**, **royalty**) has feelings (**opposites attract**, **unrequited love**) for the doctor (**protector**).

Several times the doctor, the prince, and the magistrate are separated then **reunited**.

The wife's safety is dependent on the bodyguard betraying information about the prince. They have taken (**kidnapped**) his pregnant wife into the queen's private residence along with other late-stage pregnant women.

The women don't know that the queen is waiting for one of them to deliver a boy so that she may use that child as her own (**fake relationship**, **mistaken identity**, **red herring**).

Seo-bi recovers the personal diary of her **boss' mentor physician** who had discovered how to create zombies with the **resurrection plant** (**MacGuffin**); his actions indirectly caused the King to be infected (**victim**).

The magistrate refuses to carry out the queen's order to kill the villagers (**redemption**).

In the end, the baby's mother (**return to hometown**) serves in the royal household as a **servant** to be near her son (**family**, **mistaken identity**). The prince and Seo-bi with **another protector** go on a **quest** all over Korea looking for more resurrection plants.

How the **blackmail trope** is used in Kingdom: The **blackmail** includes the prince's loyal **bodyguard** reporting to the prince's nemesis, the chief councilor. The **bodyguard** is being blackmailed with his pregnant wife's safety which is why he betrays the prince although it breaks his heart. It's a powerful storyline though it doesn't take much screen time.

The Con

Midsommar (2019)

A con is a falsehood that is successfully pedaled as the truth.

Trope Synopsis *Midsommar*:

Dani and Christian are a college-student couple (**opposites attract**, **professions**) but Christian lacks the courage to end the relationship (**fake relationship**). He feels guilty because **loner Dani** recently lost her **family** to a murder-suicide by her sister (**scar, violence**).

Instead of breaking up with her, Christian invites her (**second chance**) on a last-minute **road trip** to a rural Swedish **fairy tale** folk festival with him and his **best friends**. They arrive in Sweden all (**fish out of the water**) except for Pelle (**protector**) who is from Sweden and harbors a crush on Dani (**unrequited love**).

Loner, **orphan**, Dani is a **tortured heroine** before they even get to the festival campsite (**forced proximity**).

And it's only going to get worse for her and everyone else.

Arriving at the festival campsite, the residents (**hidden identity**, **antagonists**) treat them, and another couple also attending the festival warmly (**fake relationship**). They are offered drugs and Dani has severe hallucinations of seeing her dead family (**time travel**). The residents (**suspects**) are vague about the festival details (**secrets**). Two of Christian's **friends** want to use the festival for graduate school research. They learn of a forbidden book to outsiders which is full of details; naturally, they want it (**MacGuffin**).

Later, everyone gathers together for a ritual (**red herring**, **reunion**). But the visitors are shocked when a residential elderly couple throws themselves off a cliff to suicide (**violence**) as everyone cheers. The visitors learn that this is part of the festival but it's not all the crucial information (**con**, **secrets**). There are plenty of **politics** within the resident and student groups as well as between them. Every ninety years, nine people (**victims**) are sacrificed (**ticking time bomb**) for this ritual.

No longer a **road trip**; now the visitors are on a **quest** to survive because they are **stranded** in this bizarre **violent** ritual (**fish out of water**).

As the visitors' numbers dwindle, the visiting students turn on each other (**politics**). Christian's friends are killed (**stalked**) over their attempts to steal the **secret** book. The couple who arrived at the festival with them disappears (**victims**). He and Dani are separated by an upcoming rite. At this event, **ugly duckling** Dani is crowned May Queen (**boss**). She (**antagonist**) decides Christian will be victim #9. It's **revenge** for the discovery that Christian had sex with a **virgin**. Christian is **kidnapped** and then burned alive while Dani smiles (**ugly duckling**).

How **the con** is used in *Midsommar:* The **con** is used like a **MacGuffin** in this story. Instead of being a material object, the mystique of the festival, the guests' assumptions that it is harmless, and the residents' false assurances serve to lure **victims** to this event.

At its core movies are about cool things that happen.

But there is a relationship dynamic that is unraveled throughout.

It is not the only thing that's unraveled, often 2 or 3 things,

but by the end we have an understanding of the relationship we didn't have before.

Domestic Staff/Maid/Nanny/Droid

Raised by Wolves Season 1 (2020, HBO)

Domestic staff (**nannies**, **maids**, **housekeepers**) literally do the heavy lifting for their employers.

Trope Synopsis *Raised by Wolves*:

Set in the 22nd century after a human conflict between two groups has destroyed the earth (**violence**), two androids named Mother and Father (**domestic staff**, **protectors**) must raise six children (**family**) on a hostile, distant planet (**forced proximity**).

Five of the six children (**fish out of water**) perish from the planet's harsh conditions despite the excellent care the androids provide (**protectors**). Mother believes that the remaining son, Campion (**loner**) is the Chosen One (**mistaken identity**, **secret heir**).

Mother, Father, and Campion are atheists; they do not believe in any god. Meanwhile, a shipload of god-worshipping humans known as Mirthraics arrive in the planet's orbit (**quest**). These two groups are former earth enemies (**across the tracks, antagonists**). Scared that the Mithraic will take Campion away from the desolate planet, Mother (**boss**) crashes the ship but not before **kidnapping** five Mithraic children (**orphans**) to replace her perished offspring.

To escape earth, two atheists Sue and Marcus, murder (**violence**) two Mithraics and assume their identities (**disguise**) only to discover their victims had a school-aged son, Paul (**fake relationship**), who also thinks he's the Chosen One (**mistaken identity, secret heir**).

The orphans are shocked to discover they are living with atheists (**forced proximity**), as they've been taught to treat them as enemies (**antagonists**). Gradually, they see they are caring even if they're not believers, but they wish to remain Mithraics (**ugly duckling**). One of them, a young woman (**tortured heroine**), has become pregnant (**accidental pregnancy**) as a result of rape (**scars, violence**) by a Mithraic priest. Paul and Campion become **best friends**. Mother is supportive of the pregnant woman because she would love to become a mother herself despite it not being in her programming (**family, protector**).

Mother and Father are worried about increasing attacks by creatures (**antagonists**) that could harm the children. Mother discovers these monsters are former humans who have devolved on the planet (**mistaken identity, secrets**).

Meanwhile, the Mithraics mistake Marcus for having the favor of their god (**mistaken identity**, **red herrings**). **Politics** within the Mithraics leads to a change of leadership (**violent**). Sue takes a **road trip** to free Paul from the atheists.

Mother attacks the Mithraics and the Mithraics attack the atheists (**revenge**, **suspects**, **victims**, **violence**).

Mother doesn't remember her creation (**amnesia**) but is troubled by dreams (**time travel**). She uses the wreckage from the crashed ship to access more memories (**the con**) while saying she is on patrol. She discovers she is pregnant (**accidental pregnancy**), even though the circumstances of her pregnancy are not clear given she's an android (**secrets**). Father has an **unrequited love** for Mother.

Mother is shocked (**scar**) to give birth by vomiting up a large flying snake which flies away (**ugly duckling**, **secret baby**). She doesn't tell anyone but Father what happened (**red herrings**, **secrets**). Now the baby is terrorizing another colonist group, so Mother (**protector**) promises to kill it. But she is unable to; it escapes (**stalker**, **ticking time bomb**).

After deactivating him over a disagreement, Mother turned Father back on so that they can work together (**second chance**) to take care of the children (**family**, **protectors**). Plus, she needs his help to deal with the flying snake baby (**hidden identity**, **fake relationship**).

Sue and Marcus try to be good parents to Paul to make up for killing his parents (**redemption**). Campion, Father, and Mother all work together again (**reunion**) as the first season ends.

How the **domestic servant trope** is used in *Raised by Wolves*: As the androids are the **domestic servants**, the expectation that they would be cold is twisted into showing them more selfless than imagined up to a point. In contrast, the Mithraics' leader doesn't want to search for the missing children. And Paul is surprised by "his parents" sudden interest in him. The complexity of Mother and Father's feelings about their charges and each other is a wonderful twist—the androids are more loving and devoted parents than the humans.

Fake Relationship

Carrie (1976)

Something about this relationship isn't genuine. The power of trope comes from knowing who has that knowledge, what is the purpose of the lie, and how it will be revealed.

Trope Synopsis *Carrie*:

For some of us, high school was hell; unfortunately, that is true for Carrie too. High school (**politics**, **workplace**) is one big, **forced proximity** trope that for Carrie (**loner**, **tortured heroine**, **virgin**) only gets more suffocating. Carrie's shy and naïve nature (**fish out of water**) makes her an easy target for the school bully, Chris (**across the tracks**, **antagonist**, **boss**, **stalker**) when Carrie gets her first period in the locker room. Chris and the other girls (**suspects**) torment her bewilderment (**victim**). The gym teacher (**boss**, **protector**) tries to help Carrie but inadvertently makes things worse.

Later, one of the girls feels guilty about the bullying so she makes her boyfriend ask Carrie to the prom (**redemption**). Carrie is suspicious about the offer, fearing yet another opportunity to be shamed at her expense (**secrets**). But eventually, she is persuaded (**second chance**) partly because the gym teacher encourages her (**red herring**).

Carrie's home is no refuge because her mentally-ill mother (**family**) is openly **antagonistic** toward her. She shames Carrie and locks her in a closet for getting her period (**victim, violence**). On top of all of this, Carrie discovers her developing supernatural powers (**secrets, ticking time bomb**) which allow her to move objects with her mind (**ugly duckling**).

Meanwhile, Chris is forbidden to attend prom (**jealousy**) because she bullied Carrie so she plots elaborate **revenge** (**secrets**). The plan involves butchering pigs, their blood, and the school prom (**victims, violence**).

Carrie's mother refuses to allow Carrie to attend the prom (**boss, family**). Carrie desires her mother's permission, but her mother won't relent (**scar**). Carrie's emotions activate her telekinesis, moving household objects and finally forcing her mother to bed (**revenge, violence**).

At the prom, her **fake-relationship** date discovers he likes Carrie. She blossoms under his attention (**fish out of water**) and enjoys herself (**red herring**). The ever-present gym teacher (**mentor**) reassures Carrie about her new experiences. The other kids are friendly with her.

After dancing and even sharing the first kiss with her date, the couple is named prom king and queen (**fairy tale, ugly duckling**).

But Chris has rigged the voting (**hidden identity**) so that Carrie wins homecoming queen (**the con**). With Carrie (**woman in peril**) on the stage (**fish out water, stranded**), Chris (**stalker**) dumps the pigs' blood bucket on her (**tortured heroine, victim**) from above in the gym.

In her shock, Carrie (**victim**) unleashes her powers at the prom by locking the doors (**forced proximity**). Thinking everyone is involved in humiliating her (**red herring**), she kills all the students (**mistaken identity, victims, violence**). Afterward, while she is walking home (**road trip**), Chris and her boyfriend hit Carrie with their car. But she uses her power to kill them (**suspects, revenge**).

At home, Carrie is sitting in the bath when her mother appears (**forced proximity**). Her mother (**stalker**) is convinced Carrie (**victim**) is a witch, so she stabs her in the back (**violence**). Carrie kills her, sets the house on fire, and dies.

How does the **fake relationship trope** work in *Carrie*: Carrie tolerated her mother and the school bully's scorn. But her agony was intensified by being betrayed by those who she thought cared for her (gym teacher, date). The extra fuel of the **fake relationship** is the feeling of betrayal.

Family

Psycho (1960)

Family: can't live with 'em, can't live without 'em.

Trope Synopsis *Psycho*:

Marion steals (**hidden identity**) a large sum of money (**MacGuffin, ticking time bomb**) so that she and her boyfriend, Sam, can get married (**second chance**). On her way (**road trip**) to Sam's home, she stops at a motel (**forced proximity**).

Norman, the motel owner (**protector**) checks Marion in, who has meanwhile hidden the money she stole (**secret**). As she is the only guest, Norman invites her to have dinner with him (**forced proximity, woman in peril**). Marion regrets stealing the money. Norman admits to feeling trapped by his mother. She hears Norman arguing behind closed doors and he tells her his mother is ill (**fake relationship, hidden identity**).

Later that night, Norman's mother (**antagonist**, **stalker**) attacks Marion (**woman in peril**) in the shower, stabbing her. Norman is shocked to find Marion's corpse (**victim**). He hides her body in a car which he sinks in a pond (**secret**).

Meanwhile, Sam, Marion's sister, and a private investigator are wondering where she is (**secret**). Norman didn't realize that he sank the missing money in the pond with her (**hidden identity**, **MacGuffin**). The PI checks out all the nearby hotels including Norman's. He says she hasn't been there, but the PI recognizes her sister's handwriting in the ledger under a false name (**mistaken identity**). Norman admits that she was a guest for only one night and his mother didn't care for her (**the con**). The PI wants to talk to his mother, but Norman says she's too ill and can't be disturbed (**fake relationship**).

Later, the PI sneaks back to the motel, snooping around (**secrets**). He is caught by Noman's mother who stabs him to death (**suspect**, **woman in peril**). When the PI doesn't return on time, Sam visits the motel but only finds a silhouette of an older woman (**mistaken identity**). He returns to the town where he and Marion's sister report to the sheriff. They learn that Norman's mother has been dead for ten years (**fake relationship**, **secrets**), having died in a murder-suicide with her lover (**scars, violence**).

Back at the motel, Norman fears all the people snooping around is too much for his mother's health (**secrets**).

Although they have a big argument, he carries her down to the cellar (**forced proximity**).

Sam and Marion's sister check in to the hotel as a married couple (**hidden identity**, **red herring**). They search Marion's old room (**secret**), and her sister wants to talk to Norman's mother. Sam distracts Norman (**red herring**). Norman becomes suspicious and they fight, knocking Sam on the head (**victim**, **violence**). Lila meanwhile happens upon the unlocked cellar door.

Creeping across the floor, she calls to the woman (**red herring**, **suspect**) in the corner. Up close she realizes it is an old corpse (**hidden identity**, **victim**). Her screams alert another older woman with a knife to arrive, trapping her inside the cellar (**mistaken identity**).

Just then, a revived Sam disarms the older woman; in the confusion her wig falls off to reveal Norman (**hidden identity**, **violence**).

We learn Norman has killed his mother (**unrequited love**, **secrets**) and her lover because he was jealous of his mother's shared affections.

How the **family trope** is used in *Psycho:* Norman's mother looms larger than life over him and us in the story. The realization that she is long dead, and the depth of Norman's delusions show how far he is going to preserve his fantasy. It's not a friend or colleague that has him doing all this; it's all about his relationship with his mother.

Fish Out of Water

Shaun of the Dead (2004)

Fish Out of Water refers to a character who is in an unfamiliar situation. That creates tension because the character doesn't have other options but to operate in these new challenging circumstances.

Trope Synopsis *Shaun of the Dead*:

Slacker salesman Shaun (**profession**, **workplace**) lives with his **best friend** Ed and another roommate. Shaun's immaturity causes his girlfriend Liz (**opposites attract**) to break up with him. He (**tortured hero**) and Ed get drunk in a pub, pass out, and wake up to discover a zombie apocalypse (**antagonist**, **stalker**, **ticking time bomb**) that has struck London. Shaun (**protector**) and Ed rescue (**road trip**, **fish out of water**) Liz and Shaun's mother (**family**, **woman in peril**), all while fighting off zombies (**violence**). However, they discover acting like zombies (**disguise**) fools them (**the con**) into leaving them alone.

They rescue Shaun's abusive stepfather (**antagonist**, **family**) who has been bitten by a zombie (**ugly duckling**, **victim**). Before he dies, his stepfather apologizes to Shaun for treating him badly (**redemption**).

Also, they rescue Liz's two roommates, David and Dianne, before taking refuge in their neighborhood bar (**forced proximity**, **stranded**). Shaun's mother has been bitten (**ugly duckling**, **victim**), but she finally approves of Shaun's relationship with Liz (**redemption**).

David tries to shoot Shaun's mother, but Shawn fights him off (**second chance**). He accuses David of being in love with Liz (**forced proximity**, **jealousy**, **love triangle**, **secrets**). Dianne confirms Shaun's suspicions (**fake relationship**). By now, his mom has become a zombie, forcing Shaun (**orphan**, **scar**) to shoot her.

More zombies attack, killing Diane and David (**victims**). Shaun's third roommate appears as a zombie and Shaun (**protector**) kills him. Only Shaun, Liz, and Ed remain (**stranded**). Ed (**best friend**, **victim**) holds off the zombies while Shaun and Liz escape as the **military** arrives killing all the zombies.

Half a year later, the zombie threat is contained, with the remaining zombies being used as labor (**politics**). Shaun and Liz move in together (**return to hometown**, **reunion**). Zombie Ed (**loner**, **kidnapped**) lives in Shaun's shed (**forced proximity**, **reunion**, **secret**, **ugly duckling**) where Shaun is his **protector**.

How the **fish out of water trope** is used in *Shaun of the Dead*: This trope is a change trope with plenty of conflict for Shaun which helps him grow into a **protector**. **Fish out of water** works well with any kind of **road trip/quest**.

Heist

The Invisible Man (2020)

A **Heist** is a theft of an unusual object with a high value.

Trope Synopsis *Invisible Man*:

A tortured heroine, architect (**profession**) Cecilia is trapped in an abusive (**secret**, **violence**) relationship with her optics **billionaire** boyfriend Adrian (**family**, **suspect**). One night, she escapes their house by drugging (**con**) him and getting help from her sister (**family**). She flees (**second chance**) to stay with her **cop best friend** and his **family**.

As a result of her departure, Adrian kills himself (**victim**, **violence**). His lawyer brother (**family**, **profession**, **protector**) informs Cecilia that she has been left five million dollars.

Cecilia suspects he faked his death (**con**, **fake relationship**) because her objects are moved at home (**woman in peril**). She feels she's being **stalked** even in her friend's house. No one believes her (**tortured heroine**) theory that Adrian is **stalking** her in an invisible suit (**MacGuffin**) he created in his lab.

When Cecilia is falsely suspected of hitting her **best friend's daughter** (**mistaken identity**, **fake relationship**), she is abandoned (**loner**). She starts investigating on her own (**quest**), finding Adrian's phone (**red herring**) in her friend's house. She also reveals a **hidden** figure following her by covering it in paint. They fight but she escapes (**second chance**).

She returns to Adrian's house where she finds another invisible suit (**MacGuffin**) in his lab. She hides it in her closet (**heist**) at the house (**red herring**, **secret**) but immediately after that she is attacked (**violence**) yet escapes again (**second chance**). She meets her sister (**family**) in a restaurant (**forced proximity**); however, the invisible figure (**antagonist**) frames her (**mistaken identity**, **suspect**) for the murder of her sister (**victim**, **violence**).

Cecilia is sent to a psychiatric institution (**fish out of water**) as a result of the trial. While there, she discovers she is pregnant (**accidental pregnancy**). Her lawyer brother-in-law tells her Adrian sabotaged (**con**) her (**victim**) birth control pills. He promises to get her released if she goes back to Adrian (**blackmail**), confirming Cecilia's suspicion Adrian faked his death (**con**). Later, she fakes her suicide (**con**, **fake relationship**, **violence**), triggering the invisible figure (**antagonist**) to stop her. She stabs him with a stolen pen, puncturing a hole in the suit (**MacGuffin**, **revenge**). The figure (**antagonist**) flees the psychiatric hospital with Cecilia **stalking** him. He (**suspect**) threatens to harm her loved ones (**victims**, **violence**) in retaliation (**revenge**).

Cecilia (**tortured heroine**) arrives at her best friend's house as the figure (**suspect**) is attacking him and his daughter (**victims**, **violence**). Using her friend's gun, she (**protector**) kills the figure (**suspect**). When he is unmasked, it's revealed to be her brother-in-law (**mistaken identity**).

Searching Adrian's house, the police find Adrian hostage (**kidnapped**) in his basement. He swears he is his brother's **victim** (**fake relationship**, **red herring**) and the whole experience has made him a swell guy (**ugly duckling**).

With the now-dead Tom blamed for her sister's murder (**red herring**, **mistaken identity**), Cecilia's murder charges are dropped (**redemption**). She promises to return (**fake relationship**) to Adrian (**suspect**) if he confesses to killing her sister (**bet**) while she is secretly wearing a police wire.

While at Adrian's house, he refuses to confess. Cecilia leaves the room. While she is gone; he cuts his own throat (**violence**).

Cecilia returns, frantically calling 911 as Adrian (**suspect**) bleeds out. Yet turned away from the security camera, she motions to him (**red herring**) that she used the spare hidden suit to kill him (**hidden identity**, **revenge**).

By the time police arrive, Adrian is dead. Her story matches what is captured on his security cameras (**con**). Her **best friend** doesn't stop her from taking the invisible suit when she leaves (**redemption**).

How the **heist trope** is used in *The Invisible Man:* Cecilia steals a suit that her tormentor **stalked** her with to kill him. She makes sure he knows it's her and she creates a strong alibi. It's my kind of **heist**. It's a twist on what tends to be a pretty straightforward trope such as in *Army of the Dead*.

Holiday

Rare Exports (2009) Amazon

Trope Synopsis *Rare Exports*:

It's Christmas time in northern Finland; a **loner** Finnish boy, Pietari gets bullied by **his best friend** at a young age. Anxious to be included, Pietari and his friend, sneak across to a prohibited blasting site (**across the tracks**) from their arctic village (**forced proximity**). They spy on a **billionaire boss** running a mining operation in search of a mysterious treasure (**MacGuffin**).

At home, the boy and his **widowed butcher father** are struggling with the approaching Christmas **holiday** (**ticking time bomb**) after the death of the boy's mother (**scar**). Added to this is the loss of the annual reindeer round-up by wolves (**antagonists**) which the village depends on for survival (**politics, violence**). The boy's **best friend blackmails** him into silence about tres-passing and damaging the fence. Later, through a book in his room, the boy learns (**quest**) about the vengeful

Christmas demon (**antagonist**) that haunted the north arctic long ago (**fairy tale, time travel**). He rigs his room with toys at any entry point, trying to protect himself from his demon **stalker** (**hidden identity**). He realizes the "treasure" (**MacGuffin**) being excavated by the billionaire is the same demon (**antagonist, time travel**) in the book. He suspects demons are **stalking** him, but he keeps his theory to himself (**secret, tortured hero**).

When his father's wolf trap accidentally kills a mysterious humanoid (**fish out of water**), the father and his **best friend** quickly hide it in his butcher shop (**secret, workshop**). When the boy wanders into the workshop eating a Christmas cookie, his presence (and the cookie scent) revives the demon (**hidden identity, ugly duckling**). They discover an ID on the demon belonging to one of the billionaire's workers (**mistaken identity**) and plan to ransom the mute stranger (**MacGuffin**) back to help with the loss of the reindeer herd debt (**scar**). Meanwhile, Pietari notices all his village friends (**victims**) have gone missing (**kidnap**), along with a bunch of appliances. But the adults are too busy dealing with possible large-scale theft in their remote village to listen to Pietari's concerns (**secrets**).

The exchange doesn't go as planned. Pietari, his father, and his best friend's father meet the billionaire who plans to use the demon for his benefit (**revenge**).

A shootout occurs, the billionaire dies, and the three villagers discover what's behind airplane hangar door number one—a massive demon with the village children tied up in burlap sacks (**secrets**, **violence**). When the thawing demon emerges from his icy slumber (**ticking time bomb**), he must eat right away.

The adults set the dynamite charges into the block. They blow the demon up before he has a chance to thaw completely (**red herring**). But that's not the end of the problem; there are still scores of lesser humanoid demons running around the area.

The three villagers free the children immediately (**reunion**). Pietari (**protector**) devises a plan (**bet/wager**) to save the village (**redemption**); he will lure the demons into the electrified reindeer corrals using himself as bait (**the con**, **fish out of water**, **forced proximity**).

With their master Christmas demon destroyed, the minor demons have no memory of wanting to harm children (**amnesia**). Instead, the boy and his father (**reunion**) go into the lucrative rare export business shipping these now benign original Nordic spirits around the world (**second chance**, **return to hometown**).

How the **holiday trope** is used in *Rare Exports*: The Christmas holiday plays a central role in the setup of this movie; digging up a Christmas demon in July just isn't the same. It's the urgency that it adds working as a **ticking time bomb** trope. But also, the emotional aspect as it reminds us and the characters that Christmas comes with many memories.

Jealousy

The Fly (1986)

The grass is always greener trope.

Trope Synopsis *The Fly*:

Scientist Seth (**loner**, **profession**) meets journalist Ronnie (**profession**) at a **workplace** party. Seth demonstrates his invention (**MacGuffin**) which teleports inanimate objects to impress Ronnie. It works; they start dating (**friends to lovers**).

Seth progresses with work on his invention, solving an early problem (**ticking time bomb**) so he can teleport living tissue (**redemption**). When Ronnie leaves to meet up with her ex-lover boss, Seth is **jealous**. Meanwhile, Ronnie confronts her boss about his attempted **blackmail** about the Seth project because of his **jealousy** (**antagonist**, **secrets**).

Unwilling to trust Ronnie, Seth teleports himself alone to her apartment, yet doesn't realize a fly is in the pod with him (**forced proximity**, **hidden identity**). As far as he's concerned, everything worked fine (**ticking time bomb**). Ronnie has no idea that he visited her place.

Seth starts changing mentally and physically (**fish out of water**, **ugly duckling**). Ronnie is concerned (**woman in peril**) but he ignores her worries. She breaks up Seth's fling with another woman (**love triangle**).

He realizes his mistake with the teleporter is causing him to become a fly-human hybrid (**tortured hero**, **ugly duckling**). He creates a new program trying to reverse the effects (**scar**). Ronnie learns that she is pregnant (**accidental pregnancy**, **secret baby**). She asks her **boss** (**protector**) for help terminating the pregnancy fearing it is a monster (**suspect**, **victim**). Seth learns of her plan (**stalks**) and **kidnaps** her. He wants her to give birth to his **secret heir** (**family**). Her **boss** (**protector**) attempts to rescue Ronnie but Seth attacks him and stops just short of killing him because of Ronnie (**jealousy**, **love triangle**, **revenge**, **violence**).

Seth plans to fuse himself, Ronnie, and their unborn baby into one creation (**violence**) using his new program. She resists, they struggle, and he traps her in the pod (**stranded**).

Her **boss** (**protector**) manages to sever Ronnie's pod cables (**second chance**). Seth's pod goes awry making him even more tragic (**victim**). He begs her (**reunion**) to shoot him (**victim**) with the gun from her boss. She does (**violence**).

How is the **jealousy trope** used in *The Fly*: Seth's **jealousy** provides a humanizing aspect to his otherwise overwhelming scientific dedication. His **jealousy** when he falsely suspects his girlfriend is cheating, provides the tipping point for disaster when he risks everything to climb in a pod. With a fly.

Kidnapped

Army of the Dead (2021)

Theft of a person or other inanimate object.

Trope Synopsis *Army of the Dead*:

Loner Scott is a **widowed military** officer. He's hired by a Vegas casino **billionaire boss** to get (**quest**) his fortune (**MacGuffin**) trapped inside the vault at his casino (**forced proximity**, **workplace**). And Vegas is now run by zombies (**antagonists**).

Scott puts together a crew to help with this task for a share of the reward (**bet/wager**). They have to work quickly (**fish out of water**) because the U.S. government is going to drop nukes on Vegas (**ticking time bomb**) to purge the population soon. Also, Scott (**tortured hero**) reconnects with his estranged daughter (**family**), Kate, who blamed him for her mother's death as a zombie (**second chance**).

Now, Kate works in a refugee camp (**workplace**) outside Vegas. One of her **friends** snuck into Vegas trying to make some money for her **family**. She hasn't come back; Kate goes with Scott's team to find her (**quest**).

Once they all cross over in Vegas, their guide Lilly explains that not all zombies are the same. There are the smart Alpha zombies versus regular zombies (**across the tracks**, **politics**, **secrets**). A guard (**victim**) is sacrificed to move more easily about the city, but he was **suspected** of harming camp refugees.

While the team fans out to complete various parts of their mission, two of them (**hidden identity**) meet the zombie queen. She is killed and her head is cut off (**violence**). Now, the King of the Alpha Zombies attacks the casino (**forced proximity**) in **revenge** against Scott's crew because he has learned his queen was pregnant (**secret baby**). A few crew members die.

Unaware of all this, Kate (**woman in peril**) decides to go look for her missing friend and gets **kidnapped**. Scott wants to go after her but one of the team members is a traitor (**fake relationship**, **secrets**). The traitor wants the zombie queen's head (**MacGuffin**) because that is worth more than the vault (**politics**); the fortune was a **red herring**. Also, the U.S. government moves up the Vegas clear strike to one and a half hours away (**ticking time bomb**). Kate finds her **friend**, but she is killed (**victim**, **violence**).

The zombie queen's head is smashed, ruining the traitor's (**suspect's**) plan. He dies along with the other team members (**victims**) until only Lilly and Ward (**protector**) remain. The zombie king alpha attacks Ward (**revenge**) and bites him (**ticking time bomb**). Ward gives all the money to Kate (**reunion**), telling her to start a new life (**second chance**). Kate (**scars**) kills Ward (**victim**, **violence**) before he becomes a zombie. Kate (**orphan**) escapes (**redemption**). One remaining member who escaped Vegas is on a flight out of the U.S. when he discovers he has been bitten (**ticking time bomb**).

How the **kidnapped trope** is used in *Army of the Dead*: When the hero's daughter is **kidnapped** that throws off Scott's plan. In story terms, it adds more pressure (**conflict**) to the story because now he has to save her *and* complete the **heist**. For writers that means we have more ways to make these characters' lives harder and see how they choose to act.

Loner

Candyman (1992)

A **loner** is code for someone who doesn't pay much attention to society's rules. While admirable in a hero, it's generally creepy in antagonists.

Trope Synopsis *Candyman*:

Graduate student Helen (**loner**, **professional**, **tortured heroine**, **woman in peril**) researches an urban legend (**fairy tale**) about the death of a 19th century slave with the help of her **best friend**.

Candyman is the spirit of that **stranded** murdered slave (**antagonist**, **politics**, **scars**, **secrets**, **time travel**). Now, he's back killing (**kidnapping**, **stalking**) residents (**revenge**, **secrets**, **victims**, **violence**) with his hook for a hand on the grounds (**forced proximity**) where he was murdered centuries before (**time travel**) which now houses low-income housing.

While investigating (**quest**), Helen discovers portals in bathroom mirrors in her building and the victims' homes (**secrets**). She's intrigued because she believes there is a human killer behind the attacks but using the Candyman legend (**antagonist**, **suspect**). She befriends a mother in the housing project who tells her more about the murders and the legend (**secrets**). Helen admires the woman's baby as she'd like to be a mother one day but there are problems with her marriage (**fake relationship**, **family**, **scar**).

Helen is attacked at the project by a man with a hook for a hand (**victim**, **violence**). She identifies him; he is **suspected** of other murders. The community is relieved to have this ordeal ended (**red herring**).

Candyman appears to Helen (**antagonist**, **suspect**). He can't survive as a legend without people believing in him now that a false suspect has been arrested (**mistaken identity**). He wants to kill Helen and have her join him in his legend (**stalker**, **violence**). She learns she is the image of his long-lost lover (**unrequited love**). She refuses so he kills her best friend plus **kidnaps** the baby of the woman she met in the housing project (**suspect**, **victim**, **violence**). He also kills the woman's dog making all these murders and the kidnapping look like Helen's responsibility (**mistaken identity**).

She is imprisoned but breaks out with Candyman's help (**second chance**). She rescues the **kidnapped** baby from Candyman but dies in a fire (**redemption**). After her funeral, Helen's unfaithful husband cries whispering her name five times in the bathroom mirror (**fake relationship, love triangle**). Helen comes through the mirror with her hook and kills him. She has become the new Candyman (**antagonist, returns to hometown, suspect, ugly duckling, victim, violence**).

How the **loner trope** is used in *Candyman*: It's a great twist how the **loner trope** combines with **ugly duckling** to create Helen's new identity. It is also interesting how Helen begins the story as the **protagonist** and becomes the **antagonist**.

MILITARY/SOLDIER

PREDATOR (1987)

Preparation is a good thing.

TROPE SYNOPSIS *PREDATOR*:

Dutch (**protector**, **scar**, **soldier**) assembles a team of former soldiers (**military**, **reunion**) for a Central American rescue mission (**politics**, **road trip**). Dillion, a CIA agent (**best friend**, **boss**, **secrets**), accompanies them.

Arriving in the remote jungle, the team discovers Dillon lied (**con**, **fake relationship**, **red herring**). Their job is really to thwart a Soviet invasion (**suspects**) and find the missing soldiers (**victims**) sent in to do the job (**secrets**). Instead, they discover a rebel camp (**antagonists**). Dutch's crew blows up the camp yet manages to **kidnap** one rebel **soldier**, Anna (**woman in peril**). Being in enemy territory (**fish out of water**, **forced proximity**), they take Anna with them and head back (**road trip**) to their pick-up location. En route, they discover (**scars**) murdered, mutilated soldiers (**quest**, **victims**, **violence**). **Suspects** include Soviet soldiers, wild animals, and Anna's rebels (**mistaken identity**, **red herring**). She tells Dutch her soldiers would never do that (**opposites attract**, **secrets**).

One of the soldiers catches a glimpse of something (**MacGuffin**) tracking Dutch's crew. An alien (**antagonist**) is **stalking** them, but they don't know that yet (**hidden identity**). These soldiers are **stranded** in the jungle (**forced proximity**) against an enemy they cannot see (**hidden identity**).

They try to trap/trick it as tensions flare amongst Dutch's crew (**fish out of water**). A wild boar stumbles into the trap, springing it (**red herring**). One crew member dies (**victim**), causing another panicked crew member to fire wildly (**violence**). They don't know that an alien has been wounded in the crossfire or that it seems intent on not harming Anna (**hidden identity**).

Now they decide to double down on capturing whatever group of **antagonists** is **stalking** them (**mistaken identity**).

The alien (**antagonist**) is wounded and attacks out of **revenge**. It kills all the team members except Dutch and Anna. Dutch surmises that the alien doesn't attack those without weapons (**bet**). He (**protector**) sends Anna ahead to the pickup location (**second chance**).

Dutch (**loner**) tries covering himself with mud to lower his body temp, blocking the alien's means of stalking him (**con**). He prepares more traps for it (**secrets**).

That night, he lures (**stalks**) it out to fight him. The alien wants to fight hand to hand (**bet/wager**, **violence**). They fall into a river, and the mud washes off Dutch making him easier to see (**the protagonist in peril**). He manages to outsmart the alien with his trap (**the con**) and severely injure it (**victim**). As he watches it die, it sets off a self-destruct button (**ticking time bomb**). Dutch (**tortured hero**) escapes, **reunites** with Anna and they fly away (**redemption**).

How does the **military trope** work in *Predator*: It's the backbone of this story. Everything stems from a confrontation with a force that is superior to the military. Instead of a twist, it's an example of how this trope is the story base, and everything else story-wise is built off it.

Mistaken Identity

The Purge (2013)

A deadly miscalculation.

Trope Synopsis *The Purge*:

James (**billionaire**, **boss**, **loner**, **profession**, **protector**) has locked his **family** in their home (**forced proximity**) for the next 24 hours (**ticking time bomb**) of the lawlessness (**amnesia, fish out of water**, **politics**) known as The Purge (**quest**). His daughter's boyfriend snuck inside before the alarm was set (**hidden identity**). He confronts James about his relationship with his daughter, shots are fired, and the boyfriend dies (**violence**). Meanwhile, James' son lets an injured man from outside inside for help (**mistaken identity**). An armed gang (**antagonists**, **suspects**) shows up demanding the refugee (**victim**). The family (**stranded**) debates turning him over, and they decide against it (**second chance**).

While the mob (**antagonist**) is attacking (**stalking**), the family's neighbors come to their defense (**red herring**). James is injured (**victim**) and his wife, Mary (**woman in peril**), is kidnapped by the mob.

James dies (**violence**) as the neighbors defeat the mob (**red herring**). Then Mary learns that the neighborhood (**mistaken identity**) blames (**fake relationship**, **revenge**, **scar**) their **family** for making money off them (**victims**); the neighbors (**suspects**) plan to kill them all (**victims**, **violence**).

The bloodied stranger (**ugly duckling**) reappears, **kidnapping** the neighborhood leader and freeing Mary's family (**reunion**, **second chance**).

A few hours later, the neighborhood leader (**suspect**) attacks Mary (**victim**) but she (**protector**) fends her off (**second chance**). The purge ends (**ticking time bomb**) and everyone leaves. Mary (**tortured heroine**, **widow**) is with her **family** in their home (**return to hometown**, **second chance**).

How the **mistaken identity trope** has been used in *The Purge*: The neighbors **secretly** planning to kill the family during The Purge (and when they are under siege by a gang) is such a great use of the **mistaken identity trope** and **red herring**. It swings the whole story tension up even higher because the intended **violence** is made more personal.

Opposites Attract

Eternal Sunshine of the Spotless Mind (2004)

Story conflict is better when birds of a feather, don't flock together.

Trope Synopsis *Eternal Sunshine of the Spotless Mind*:

Joel (**loner**, **tortured hero**) decides to have his memories erased (**amnesia**) of his relationship with Clementine (**best friends**, **opposites attract**) when he realizes that she has erased all thoughts of him (**revenge**). Joel tries to hold onto his memories of Clementine as he seeks to erase them (**quest**). The **ticking time bomb** is that he will completely forget her as soon as the techs have completed the sessions (**forced proximity**).

Two techs (**antagonists**) at the memory erasure business (**workplace**) delete Joel's memories despite his ambivalence to erase them. One of them (**hidden identity**) uses Joel's memories to try to seduce (**fake relationship**)

Clementine in the present (**love triangle**). The memory company's **boss** had an affair (**secret**) with one of his employees. The employee had her memories of their relationship erased (**amnesia**). But when she learns about it, she sends (**revenge**) all the company records (**secrets**) to the victims who had their memories erased (**second chance**). Joel and Clementine realize that there is good in relationships as well as pain (**reunion**).

How the **opposites attract trope** is used in *Eternal Sunshine of the Spotless Mind*: This trope is the foundation of the story. It's what pulls these two characters together and what splits them apart. All the other tropes are built off **opposites attract**. This movie gets extra points from me for the interesting use of the **amnesia** trope too.

Professions

The Witch (2015)

Everyone has a job to do.

Trope Synopsis *The Witch*:

In the 17th century, a **family's** conflict (**politics**) with their religious community (**workplace**) causes them to be expelled (**stranded**). Life on their own at the edge of a sinister forest means they are struggling to survive (**fish out of water**). Then, the family's new baby (**victim**) disappears (**kidnapped**) when their oldest daughter Tomasin (**protector**) is watching it. In this Puritan family, whispers of the devil's presence begin (**antagonist**).

Meanwhile, the father (**boss**) has pawned a valuable antique of the mother's for supplies (**MacGuffin**) without her knowledge (**secrets**). Its disappearance (**red herring**) causes the mother, in her grief (**scars**), to suspect her young adult daughter Tomasin (**mistaken**

identity, **fake relationship**). The mother wishes to send her away to work for another family (**domestic servant**, **ticking time bomb**).

The children hear this plan (**secrets**) and Tomasin **blackmails** her brother into taking her with him into the forest for hunting (**road trip**). Once inside, Tomasin falls and is knocked unconscious (**amnesia**), the family dog runs off, and her brother is seduced by a beautiful witch (**fake relationship**, **hidden identity**).

Her father finds Tomasin, her brother, and the disemboweled dog in the forest (**reunion**, **violence**). Back home, the mother blames Tomasin (**mistaken identity**, **suspect**) for leading her brother (**victim**) into the forest. The father confesses he sold her precious antique (**secrets**), not Tomasin (**victim**).

Meanwhile, her brother vomits up an apple with a bite taken out of it (**fairy tale**, **secrets**). Tomasin observes her younger **twin** siblings talking to the family's black billy goat (**secrets**). When she questions them about it, they accuse her of witchcraft (**fake relationship**, **mistaken identity**). Tomasin (**woman in peril**) milks the nanny goat and finds blood on her hands (**red herring**).

Later, her brother dies (**scar**). The twins refuse prayer (**scar**). The father accuses Tomasin (**tortured heroine**) of witchcraft. She defends her belief that the goat is the devil, and she is innocent (**victim**) against his accusations.

Distraught with suspicions of witchcraft, her father locks Tomasin and the twins (**suspects**) in the goat house for the night (**forced proximity**). The three children see a witch (**stalker**) drinking blood from the nanny goat; the witch attacks the twins (**stranded**). Meanwhile, the mother admits she had an affair (**love triangle**), and their missing baby was the product of that union. The mother has a dream (**time travel**) about her dead son and missing baby. When she awakes in the morning her breasts are bloody from animal bites (**violence**).

The father opens the goat house in the morning to find Tomasin's hands are bloody, the twins have disappeared, and the goats are dead (**violence**). Then the billy goat (**antagonist**, **hidden identity**) kills the father before Tomasin. Her mother appears and blames everything on Tomasin for being a witch (**mistaken identity**, **tortured heroine**, **suspect**). She (**loner**) denies all the accusations while fighting her mother off in self-defense before killing her (**victim**, **violence**, **second chance**).

Tomasin (**orphan**) finds the billy goat (**antagonist**), asking him what has happened. He transforms into a man (**boss**, **ugly duckling**), asking her to be a witch (**profession**). Tomasin follows him into the forest to join the coven (**family**), finding a place to belong at last (**redemption**).

How is the **profession trope** used in *The Witch*: The false accusations of Tomasin being a witch eventually drive her to accept that **profession** in the end. Good twist of the **profession** trope.

Quest/Journey

Bird Box (2018) Netflix

A life-changing search.

Trope Synopsis *Bird Box*:

Malorie (**tortured heroine**, **protector**) tells her two young children, named Boy and Girl, they must prepare for a river trip (**quest**) with her where they all must be blindfolded (**fish out of water**) to avoid seeing the deadly entities (**antagonists**, **suspects**). They take her pet birds (**protectors**) as warning devices for when the entities are nearby.

Flashback (**time travel**) to five years ago: a pregnant (**loner**) Malorie and her sister (**family**) are visiting the doctor's office for a check-up. They are interrupted by a news report of mass suicides abroad (**ticking time bomb**). After leaving the appointment, they witness a woman killing herself (**scar**, **violence**).

While driving, her sister crashes the car then jumps out in front of a truck and dies (**violence**). Malorie (**woman in peril**) runs away with others as people commit suicide all around them (**violence**). When she falls, a woman steps out of her house to help her (**second chance**). As the woman is helping her, she kills herself (**violence**). Malorie escapes inside where the woman's distraught husband (**widower**) and half a dozen others (**victims**) have taken shelter (**stranded**).

They barricade themselves inside and share information (**forced proximity**). They learn that originating in folklore (**fairy tales**) are demons, now known as entities (**stalkers**), which manifest as the person's greatest fear or loss. The group assumes the only way to avoid them is to keep their eyes closed (**bet/wager**).

Back in the present time (**time travel**), Malorie and the kids are still rowing blindfolded down the river (**quest**). She hears the entities whispering her name (**secrets**).

Flashback to five years ago (**time travel**), another pregnant woman seeks refuge in the same house (**victim, woman in peril**). One of the other refugees tries watching the outside with exterior cameras as a **bet/wager** to see if he is impacted. A short time later, he kills himself (**victim, violence**). Malorie hears a noise at night and goes to investigate, fearing an intrusion. It's only two of the residents having sex (**red herring**).

Flashback to the river: A man (**antagonist**) calls to Malorie, assuring her she can remove her blindfold (**mistaken identity**). When she refuses, he attacks her, trying to remove her blindfold (**red herring**). She kills him with her machete with her blindfold still on (**protector**).

Flashback to five years ago: the group goes out for food (**fish out of water**). Inside the store they visit, Malorie takes some birds as pets with her. They discover a **victim** is locked in the freezer, calling for help (**hidden identity**). One of the group dies inside with him when he starts breaking out so the rest of the group can escape (**second chance**). Back at the house, Malorie and the **widower** homeowner (**boss**) grieve their dead **family** members (**scars**). Two of the group take the car and escape, leaving everyone else there **stranded** without a car.

Back to the river timeline: Now Malorie has been on the river for 24 hours (**quest**). Boy gets knocked out of the boat, but she rescues him (**protector**). She hears the entity nearby whispering (**secrets**). She returns to the boat with the children, and they get back on the river (**reunion, quest**).

Back in the past, Malorie falls in love with one of the other refugees, Tom (**friends to lovers**). A new refugee (**antagonist, fake relationship, hidden identity**), enters the house, claiming to be a **victim**. His presence divides the group members (**politics**). The homeowner (**boss**) wants him gone, but instead he's locked up in his garage (**kidnapped, forced proximity**). The other pregnant woman asks Malorie to take care of her baby if something happens to her (**protector, second chance**).

Malorie gives her a stuffed animal as a baby gift and reassurance (**guardian**).

Back on the river, Girl is holding the stuffed animal Malorie gave her mom (**hidden identity**). Now we know that Girl was the other woman's child (**orphan**). The three of them decide to face the rapids with their blindfolds on rather than trying to sacrifice anyone by looking ahead (**reunion**).

Back in the past: the new resident (**mistaken identity**) pulls down window coverings and opens the garage (**antagonist**). The two women are in labor (**stranded**). Girl's mother delivers her and hands her to Malorie before jumping out the exposed window (**victim**, **violence**). Malorie (**protector**) hides with both babies (**twins**) while the homeowner, the newest resident, and another person all die in a frenzy of agony (**victims**, **violence**). Tom survives with Mallory and the babies (**reunion**).

They raise the kids together for the next five years (**family**). Humans embodied by entities start stalking them outside their house (**stalking**). A man (**guardian**) contacts Malorie and Tom, telling them he is at a safe place for them and their family. It's a long dangerous trip to get there (**quest**). They worry it's a trap, but they don't have other options (**bet/wager**).

Tom distracts the humans possessed by entities so that Malorie and the kids can escape (**red herring**). He kills some but also has his eyes exposed and kills himself (**victim**, **violence**). Malorie (**protector**, **widow**,

woman in peril) and the kids make it down to the boat, getting on the river.

Back in the present time, Malorie and the kids' boat gets upset by rapids but they all survive and continue back down the river (**second chance**). Finally, they make it to the place where they hear all the birds singing (**guardians**). The entities try to get them to take their blindfolds off (**mistaken identities**). They reach the end of the journey; the place is a school for the blind (**reunion**). Malorie releases her birds (**second chance**). She names the children Tom and Olympia (**redemption**).

How the **quest trope** is used in *Bird Box*: The **quest trope** drives both main storylines. The story remains engaging because the **quests** are different in each one but related. New information is revealed through tropes in each.

REDEMPTION

PRIDE AND PREJUDICE AND ZOMBIES (2016)

It all comes back around.

TROPE SYNOPSIS *PRIDE AND PREJUDICE AND ZOMBIES*:

The five unmarried Bennet sisters (**family**) are trained in martial arts (**protectors**) to combat zombies (**violence**) as they enter the marriage mart. When the wealthy Bingley family moves nearby (**forced proximity**), Mrs. Bennet schemes that eldest daughter Jane should marry Mr. Bingley (**arranged marriage**) once they meet at a neighborhood ball. Also present for the event is Mr. Bingley's **best friend**, Colonel Darcy. Lizzy overhears him slighting the female guests' appearances (**scar**), and instantly dislikes him (**enemies to lovers**). When a zombie (**antagonist**) hoard attacks the party, Darcy (**tortured hero**) saves Lizzy's life (**second chance**). Then he's impressed as she fiercely fights (**violence**) off the hoard (**suspects**) with her sisters (**family**).

The following day, Jane is attacked (**woman in peril**) by a zombie and is wounded (**victim**). Jane's illness brings Darcy to visit as he suspects she is becoming a zombie (**mistaken identity**, **secrets**). Lizzy rejects his interference and turns him away (**revenge**).

After Jane recovers, Bingley holds another ball (**reunion**). Here Lizzy meets Wickham (**love triangle**), who tells her about his past association with Darcy, painting him in dreadful light (**fake relationship**, **the con**). When a zombie hoard (**antagonists**) attacks the party, Lizzy and Darcy fight them off (**second chance**).

Meanwhile, Mrs. Bennet needs husbands (**victims**) for her daughters because the single clergyman, Mr. Collins (**boss**), will inherit the family home (**MacGuffin**). He first expresses interest in Jane (**unrequited love**) but Mrs. Bennet, hoping Jane and Bingley will marry soon, redirects him to Lizzy (**victim**). Mr. Collins offers to marry Lizzy (**arranged marriage**), but she will have to retire her combat skills. Lizzy refuses (**unrequited love**).

Wickham invites Lizzy to visit a restricted area where the zombies are fed animal brains to keep them from attacking humans (**forced proximity**). He asks Lizzy to marry him and leave the area, though Lizzy is unsure (**love triangle**).

She returns home to find Bingley has left the neighborhood, leaving Jane heartbroken (**scar**, **tortured hero**, **victim**). Darcy stops by and proposes to Lizzy (**opposites attract**). When she asks about Bingley, he tells her that he convinced him Jane's family was unsuitable and she didn't truly care for Bingley (**fake relationship**, **mistaken identity**). Furious at Darcy for breaking her sister's heart, she and Darcy fight (**revenge**). She bests him, and he leaves (**violence**).

Darcy sends a letter to Lizzy, apologizing for his behavior with Jane and Bingley (**second chance**). He also tells her that Wickham tried to elope (**kidnap**) his wealthy underage sister (**scars**). He had gone to London to fight the zombies who approached the city (**loner**, **protector**).

As Lizzy struggles to process all this information, Darcy's great aunt Lady Catherine De Bourgh arrives at the family home, telling her not to marry Darcy because he's marrying her sickly daughter (**love triangle**). As the zombie hoard (**antagonist**, **suspects**) approaches their neighborhood, Lady Catherine invites the family to shelter at her estate (**forced proximity**).

After arriving at the estate, Lizzy discovers her headstrong youngest sister has run off with Wickham (**fake relationship**, **red herring**). Lizzy and Jane leave the estate in search of Lydia (**quest**). Meanwhile, Darcy (**protector**) finds Wickham and Lydia (**second chance**).

Darcy and Lizzy join forces to fight the zombies at the London gate (**reunion**). Darcy stabs Wickham, revealing the zombie bite he'd been hiding by eating animal brains (**hidden identity**, **ugly duckling**). Wickham charges the stunned Darcy, but Lizzy rides by slicing off his arm (**protector**, **violence**). An explosion (**ticking time bomb**) to keep the zombies away from the gate knocks Darcy unconscious (**amnesia**). Lizzy confesses her love for him, although he can't hear her (**ugly duckling**, **unrequited love**). He wakes up and tells her he loves her too; they agree to marry (**redemption**). As the credits roll, they are interrupted by the scene of zombie Wickham leading a massive zombie army toward them (**ticking time bomb**).

How the **redemption trope** is used in *Pride and Prejudice and Zombies:* Since most of the story is driven by **red herrings**, the **redemption trope** is used in the payoff for the reveal. It's paired here with the **ugly duckling trope** for some really great story beats in the last act.

Return to Hometown/Smalltown

Nightmare on Elm Street (1984)

There's no place like home.

Trope Synopsis *Nightmare on Elm Street*:

Nancy, her **best friend**, and their boyfriends have similar dreams about a **stalker**. Her best friend dies (**victim**), and her boyfriend is arrested (**suspect**). Nancy's **father** is a **police officer** who believes the boyfriend is innocent (**victim**).

Nancy falls asleep in school where she is being chased by the **stalker**. She burns herself in the dream (**time travel**) to wake up. She has a burn mark on her arm when she awakens (**victim**, **violence**).

At home, she falls asleep in the bathtub and almost drowns (**second chance**). The **suspect** boyfriend dies in prison (**fake relationship**). In a dream with the **stalker**, Nancy steals his hat with his name, Freddie Kruger on it.

Her mother tells her Kruger (**antagonist**) was a murderer (**suspect**) who was killed by the people living on her street (**revenge**). Now he has **returned to his hometown** for **revenge** on others (**violence**). Nancy's mother locks her in the house for safety (**forced proximity**).

Nancy attempts to contact one of her other friends to warn him about Freddie but she fails to talk to him. He is killed (**victim**, **violence**) in his sleep by Freddie (**antagonist**).

Nancy hatches a plan where she **cons** Kruger into entering her world and **kidnaps** and secures him (**suspect**). She runs to get her father (**boss**). In the meantime, Kruger has escaped his confinement and is trying to kill her mother (**woman in peril**). Nancy realizes Kruger's power comes from his victim's fear (**bet/wager**). She forces herself to drop her fear and Kruger disappears (**the con**, **ugly duckling**).

Outside, her mother and her friends remain unharmed (**second chance**). Later, Nancy's car is possessed, and her mother disappears (**fake relationship**, **violence**). Freddie is hiding and waiting (**revenge**, **secrets**, **second chance**).

How the **return to hometown trope** is used in *Nightmare on Elm Street:* Usually this trope is used similarly to a **reunion trope**. It communicates a return to normalcy after the story crisis. But for *Elm Street,* it's used to generate uncertainty in the audience. Everything is safe again, or is it?

Reunion

Rosemary's Baby (1968)

Time to get the band back together.

Trope Synopsis *Rosemary's Baby*:

Loner, **tortured heroine** Rosemary and her actor husband (**family**, **profession**) move into a haunted house (**fish out of water**, **forced proximity**, **secrets**, **stranded**) in New York. Her husband, Guy, wants to be a successful actor more than anything (**quest**). Rosemary meets her new elderly neighbors at the scene of another neighbor's accidental death (**fake relationship**, **violence**). This older, wealthy couple befriends Rosemary and Guy (**across the tracks**, **age difference**, **fake relationship**, **family**, **stalkers**, **suspects**).

Rosemary doesn't know that with the help of her neighbors, Guy makes a deal with the devil that Rosemary will carry his child (**bet/wager**, **secret heir**) in exchange for him having a successful acting career (**quest**).

Rosemary (**victim**) is drugged (**amnesia**, **fairy tale**, **time travel**) and raped (**scar**, **violence**) by Guy (**antagonist**, **suspect**).

Guy insists he is the father of the baby (**con**, **hidden identity**, **fake relationship**). A variety of doctors (**antagonists**, **boss**) tell Rosemary not to worry and be compliant with what they say (**con**, **fake relationship**).

A **friend** of Rosemary's gives her a book with clues (**MacGuffin**) to her neighbor's identity before he dies (**violence**). Their neighbors are revealed to be Satan worshippers (**hidden identity**, **politics**).

Rosemary's (**tortured heroine**, **woman in peril**) health suffers as the pregnancy progresses (**quest**, **ticking time bomb**).

After the baby's birth (**quest**), the baby is cared for (**kidnapped**) by other witches and satanists (**domestic staff**) while Rosemary is drugged again.

Rosemary sees him (**hidden identity**). Other witches remark on his strange eyes (**ugly duckling**). She is encouraged to take care of the baby and begins mothering him (**opposites attract**, **protector**, **reunion**).

How the **reunion trope** is used in *Rosemary's Baby*: Throughout the movie, Rosemary's emotional and physical journey with her pregnancy is pretty horrifying. She is completely **victimized**. But in the end after the baby is taken away from her, she goes to see it. When she sees the baby, she chooses to mother the satanic baby. That choice brings her back to her original desire to be a mother.

Revenge

Scream (1996)

Payback time.

Trope Synopsis *Scream*:

It's exactly a year (**ticking time bomb**) after Sidney's (**woman in peril**, **scar**) mother's murder (**family**, **violence**) by Cotton Weary (**antagonist**, **mistaken identity**), the man Sidney identified. Sidney's father (**widower**, **family**) prepares for a road trip, leaving her alone so she plans to stay with her **best friend**, Tatum. At school (**workplace**), everyone is talking about the recent murder (**violence**, **ticking time bomb**) of another student (**victim**).

After school, while waiting for Tatum to pick her up, Sidney receives a strange taunting phone call about her mother's death. The caller (**antagonist**, **hidden identity**), wearing a black cloak and white face mask, is in her house (**forced proximity**) and attacks her (**violence**).

Sidney escapes to her bedroom, locks herself in, and calls the police (**protectors**). Billy arrives via her bedroom window as his usual entry, but Sidney **suspects** he was calling her. She flees her bedroom to find the police at her front door.

At the police station where she and Billy are taken in for questioning, she meets Dewey, the town deputy, and Tatum's older brother (**family**, **protector**). She also meets Gail (**antagonist**, **profession**), who covered Sidney's murder, who doesn't agree Cotton is the killer and is following up on this recent murder (**quest**).

Later at Tatum's house, Sidney gets another taunting phone call. This time the caller suggests Sidney's ID of her mother's killer was wrong. At school the following day, the caller/killer confronts her in the bathroom, but she flees (**stalker, ticking time bomb**).

Sidney and her friends throw a party at her empty house (**forced proximity**) because in high school the mentality is that everything is a reason for a party, even if there's a serial killer on the loose. Gail and Dewey show up and appear friendly with each other (**opposites attract**). Everyone is unaware that Tatum has been killed in the garage until the killer emerges and stabs Billy (**violence**). Chaos ensues at the party as the killer stabs Dewey. Gail accidentally runs her truck into a tree trying to escape (**woman in peril**).

Inside the house (**forced proximity**), Sidney (**woman in peril**) has locked out Billy's two friends (**suspects**). Each is claiming the other one is the killer; one wants to leave and the other wants to come inside (**red herring**). Billy stumbles downstairs with his bloody wound. He lets them both inside, shooting one immediately. Then he reveals his bloody wound is fake (**red herring**, **secret**); he and the other guy, Stu, are the white-faced killers (**antagonists**, **fake relationship**, **family**, **hidden identity**, **loner**, **stalker**, **ugly duckling**).

Billy killed Sidney's mother (**violence**) because she was having an affair (**love triangle**, **secrets**) with his father (**revenge**). He has **kidnapped** Sidney's father and plans to frame him (**revenge**) for the murders (**victims**). Billy and Stu injure each other (**scars**), trying to make it look as if their wounds were from fighting off Sidney's father (**fake relationship**).

Gail appears with Dewey's gun. She tries to shoot Billy but fails. They fight and Sidney (**stranded**, **tortured heroine**) attacks Billy's BFF killing him; then she kills Billy with Dewey's gun (**redemption**). In the end, Dewey has survived, and Gail reports the latest news story (**reunion**).

How does the **revenge trope** work in *Scream*: **Revenge** is the impetus for the story, but it gets twisted along the way. Billy kills Sidney's mother for the affair he blames ruined his **family** life. But all the other people Billy and Stu kill aren't related to the original **family** issue. His elaborate lengthy **revenge** plan for killing Sidney and her father does a nice job bringing that trope full circle.

RIVAL

CORALINE (2009)

Sometimes there can't be only one.

TROPE SYNOPSIS *CORALINE*:

Loner, **tortured heroine**, **ugly duckling** Coraline's parents (**family**, **fish out of water**, **profession**) don't have time to spend with her in their isolated new house (**forced proximity**, **secrets**). Coraline visits with her new neighbors the opera singers and the band leader (**family**, **red herrings**, **road trips**).

Bored and frustrated, Coraline finds a secret passageway to a parallel world (**time travel**) in her new house. In this new place (**across the tracks**, **fairy tale**), she meets Other Mother and Other Father who are fun, attentive, and indulgent (**fake relationship**, **mistaken identity**, **red herrings**, **twins**).

But there are warnings in Coraline's new home. She finds a doll who looks just like her (**hidden identity**, **twin**) which seems to change locations around her house. The hidden door she finds isn't always accessible by a skeleton key (**MacGuffin**). There's a black cat always skulking around as well as a boy her age named Wybie. Plus, dancing mice! They all warn her to varying degrees about the Other Mother (**secrets**), but Coraline's hurt and pride keep her from listening.

She meets a version of Wybie in the Other Mother's (**boss**) world but he, like her Other Father, is a puppet. The Other Mother (**stalker**) tells Coraline all she needs to do to stay with them is to sew buttons in her eyes (**victim**, **violence**). Coraline refuses. She sees the cat in the other world (**time travel**). He speaks to her, telling her that the Other Mother loves to play games and hates to lose. The Other Mother is shown to be a witch (**hidden identity**) who can change her form.

Coraline finds three ghosts of the Other Mother's previous victims. They warn her that she will be trapped here like them if she sews the buttons in her eyes. Back in her real life the Other Mother has **kidnapped** her parents. Coraline (**woman in peril**) challenges the Other Mother to a game (**bet/wager**). If she wins, her parents are free, and the ghost children go free. If she loses, she will sew the buttons on her eyes and stay (**ticking time bomb**).

Coraline must find three ghost eyes in each of the worlds that The Other Mother created—the garden, the opera singers, and the band leader's place. She wins the contest with the cat's help and returns home to find her parents waiting (**redemption**, **reunion**).

How the **rival trope** is used in *Coraline*: I love "The Other Mother." What a great twist on the **rival trope**. The use of **hidden identity**, **twin** and **family tropes** work so well with making Coraline's Other Mother more threatening.

Road Trip

Zombieland (2009)

Pile in; the gang's all here.

Trope Synopsis *Zombieland*:

Tortured hero, **loner**, Columbus is a Texas college student terrified of clowns who has survived the zombie apocalypse (**fish out of water**, **stranded**, **ticking time bomb**). He is **road tripping** his way back to Columbus Ohio to his parents (**family**). Along the way, he meets Tallahassee (**best friend**, **scar**, **secrets**, **victim**) who is on the hunt (**quest**) for America's last twinkie (**MacGuffin**). Tallahassee tells him (**orphan**) everyone else is dead thanks to the zombies (**antagonists**, **stalkers**).

The two guys are robbed (**the con**) at a convenience store by two sisters (**family**), Wichita (**boss**) and Little Rock, who are driving to California to find a zombie-free amusement park (**quest**).

With hurt pride, Tallahassee convinces Columbus to join him in tracking down his stolen vehicle. They meet up again with the sisters (**reunion**), agreeing to **road trip** to California.

Once in LA, they visit actor Bill Murray's home (**forced proximity**) using a map of the stars (**MacGuffin**). Little Rock is too young to know this acting legend, so they start watching Ghostbusters from his private home screening room (**red herring**). They are shocked to discover the real Bill Murray still lives there but he pretends to be a zombie when he goes out for camouflage (**second chance**, **secrets**). Columbus isn't aware of this last fact, shooting Murray thinking he is a zombie (**victim**).

Columbus and Wichita (**opposites attract**, **friends to lovers**) almost kiss. But then the sisters strike out on their own to avoid **politics**. Inside the amusement park, the girls (**women in peril**) get trapped (**stranded**) by a zombie hoard. Columbus (**protector**) has to face a zombie clown (**antagonist**) to free them. Tallahassee joins in the rescue. The four of them decide to form a **family** (**redemption**). Wichita tells Columbus her real name (**hidden identity**).

How is the **road trip trope** is used in *Zombieland*: The **road trip trope** is a mobile **forced proximity trope**. With the entire geographic USA, the story focus needed to be narrowed down to settings where the characters would be forced to interact. Zombies provided the reason behind the **forced proximity**.

Second Chance

What We Do in the Shadows Season One (2019) Hulu

Survive to fight another day.

Trope Synopsis *What We Do in the Shadows*:

Inside a gothic house (**forced proximity**, **workplace**), in present-day Staten Island, live four vampires (**age difference**, **fish out of water**, **time travel**) and their familiar (**domestic servant**), Guillermo. They are the subject of a documentary film crew, recording their undead lives. Nandoor, the oldest vampire is a former Turkish Sultan, decorated general, and de facto head of the house (**family**, **military**, **protector**, **royalty**, **secrets**, **scars**, **stalker**). The other two vampires are a married couple, Lazlo (**family**, **playboy**, **secrets**, **victim**) and his wife, Nadia (**family**, **secrets**, **stalker**). Their fourth roommate, Collin Robinson (**loner**), is an energy vampire and unaffected by daylight (**loner**). Maintaining the house and vampire livelihood is Guillermo (**best, friend, domestic servant, secrets**).

Nadia finds her reincarnated lover (**forbidden love**), Jeff, only to find her heroic lover is now a timid parking garage attendant (**amnesia, hidden identity, opposites attract, secrets**). When he finally regains his memory with Nadia's help (**reunion**), Lazlo (**jealousy, stalker, violence**) announces he has been busy chasing him (**revenge, time travel**) and decapitating him (**scars, ticking time bomb, victim**) for many lifetimes (**love triangle, protector, unrequited love, violence**). Jeff accidentally kills himself (**red herring, violence**) leaving his ghost (**antagonist**) to haunt Nadia's indifference.

All the vampires except Collin Robinson, have to contend with their European **boss**, The Baron, coming to stay with them (**road trip**). He has expectations that they are ruling the New World (**antagonist, age difference, family, fling, forced proximity, politics, red herring**). The vampires struggle to maintain **the con** that they are more powerful than they are (**ticking time bomb**). They visit a powerful vampire (**antagonist**) in NYC who disdains the vampires but is willing to help them in exchange for Lazlo's cursed hat (**MacGuffin**). Accidentally, the vampire and all his followers die after he dons the hat (**victims, violence**).

Nadia and Lazlo's ongoing search for a familiar ends with the one they like becoming a zombie. Only Guillermo notices the familiar's change, or that it fakes carrying out any duties (**mistaken identity, secrets**).

Guillermo's waiting (**tortured hero**) to become a vampire (**ugly duckling, unrequited love**). As a **domestic servant**, he has to **kidnap** new **virgin victims** for the vampires. Nadia (**age difference, mistaken identity**) decides to turn one of those potential victims, a bullied young woman (**woman in peril**), into a vampire.

Meanwhile, Lazlo befriends his football-loving human neighbor (**best friend**) but accidentally reduces his brain to mush by overdoing his **amnesia** treatment. Energy vampire Collin Robinson is surprised to find himself with a manipulative, needy girlfriend (**family**) from his **workplace** that both repels and excites him. Tired of all the house's toxic masculinity, Nadia conjures up her ghost as company and enchants her into doll form for companionship (**twin**).

Lazlo tries to help his amnesic neighbor but ends up getting caught by animal control in bat form (**forced proximity, stranded**).

Lonely Nandoor wants to meet one of his descendants (**family, quest**) so Guillermo does a DNA test on him (**red herring**). Guillermo's DNA results provide him a shock; he's descended from the Van Helsing **family** (**hidden identity, secret heir, protector, secret, ugly duckling**). In light of this reveal, the accidental death of The Baron by Guillermo (**protector**) a short time before seems less random. The Vampiric council blames the three house vampires for The Baron's death (**mistaken identity, politics**). They are sentenced to die at sunrise.

Guillermo and Collin Robinson save them (**redemption, return to hometown**).

How the **second chance trope** works in WWDIS: Having the characters escape death to live and fight another day is the staple of any series. Horror is no exception. **Second chance** is a **red herring** where we and the characters seize a new opportunity to take the story in an unexpected direction.

Secret Baby

Alien (1979)

It's the gift that keeps on giving.

Trope Synopsis *Alien*:

The Nostromo spaceship (**workplace**) is returning to earth (**return to hometown**) with its seven-person crew in stasis (**amnesia**).

The crew is awakened by the onboard computer, named Mother (**guardian**), after it detects another ship's distress call (**red herring, secrets**).

The ship lands on the nearby moon to investigate, and three crew members leave the ship (**road trip**). They find an abandoned alien ship (**stranded**) but cannot decipher the distress message further (**fish out of water, red herring**).

While exploring the ship, a crew member's face is attacked by a creature (**antagonist**). His two crewmates (**best friends**) help him back to the Nostromo with the alien stuck to his face rather than sacrifice him (**ticking time bomb**).

Back on board, the creature is found dead on the ship (**mistaken identity**, **red herring**). The crew member appears unharmed (**red herring**, **scar**) despite some **amnesia**. The crew continues back toward earth (**quest**).

Later, the crewmember dies (**victim**) when an alien escapes his chest (**antagonist**, **secret baby**, **surprise pregnancy**, **violence**). The alien (**MacGuffin**) evades capture on the ship (**forced proximity**).

After the crewmember's death, the crew **stalks** the creature (**fish out of water**). The fast-growing alien is now stronger than the humans (**across the tracks**). It begins killing the crew one by one (**secrets**, **ticking time bomb**).

With only four crew members left, the new captain, Ripley (**boss**, **guardian**, **loner**), continues trying to capture the alien (**suspect**).

Ripley discovers from Mother that their fellow crew member, Ash, is a mole (**fake relationship**, **suspect**). Ash attacks Ripley when she accuses him of treason (**revenge**). They learn Ash is an android and their employers (**billionaires**) want (**the con**, **secrets**) the alien to return to earth (**return to hometown**). Their employers (**antagonists**) don't care about the crew (**the con**). Ripley eliminates Ash.

Big Reveal / Truth hero finds.

but he is rebuffed. The reporter develops recent photographs. In every picture with the priest, a weapon hangs above his head but no one else's.

Kathy and Damien visit a zoo with disastrous results as animals react violently to the child's presence.

The priest corners Thorn. He tells him that Damien is the son of the devil, who will lead the world into chaos unless Thorn kills him. And btw, his wife is pregnant. After Thorn leaves, the priest is killed by a falling object.

Thorn goes home where his wife tells him she's pregnant (**ticking time bomb**). She's (**protector**) concerned about Damien and the baby. Thorn learns the priest died violently. He goes to investigate that. Damien (**stalker**) throws his mother down the stairs (**woman in peril**), and she miscarries (**forced proximity**, **stranded**, **victim**).

Thorn (**protector**) and the reporter travel to Rome (**road trip**), tracking down the priest (**antagonist**) who arranged the adoption. He is near death and directs them to the graves of Damien's mother (**mistaken identity**) and Thorn's baby (**fake relationship**, **hidden identity**, **kidnapped**, **scar**, **secrets**, **victims**, **violence**). They escape after a pack of dogs attacks them (**stalking**, **stranded**).

Thorn learns his wife (**woman in peril**, **victim**, **violence**) jumped to her death, but in reality, she was thrown out of a window by the nanny (**antagonist**, **jealousy**, **stalker**, **suspect**, **violence**).

Widower Thorn must travel to the middle east to get the special knives he needs to kill Damian (**MacGuffin**, **quest**). His investigative friend (**best friend**, **victim**) dies in a freak accident.

Back home, a vicious dog tries to prevent him from entering the house, but he manages to lock it away. Then he is attacked by the nanny (**revenge**, **stalker**). He is now convinced Damien is the devil's son (**secret heir**). He grabs Damien, driving him to a church (**second chance**).

Thorn dies in a shoot-out with the police before he can get Damien inside.

Damien is adopted by Thorn's brother, the U.S. president (**fake relationship**, **family**, **hidden identity**, **return to hometown**, **secret**, **ticking time bomb**, **ugly duckling**).

How is the **secret/lost hier** used in *The Omen:* It's the main plotline driving the story which is then packed with **red herrings**, **hidden identities**, and **secrets**.

Suspects

Annihilation (2018)

They're the ones to blame.

Trope Synopsis *Annihilation*:

The biologist (**profession**, **military**, **loner**, **widow**, **tortured heroine**) Lena accepts a position as part of an investigative team (**politics**) entering the Shimmer (**quest**). A few years previously, a meteorite hit the earth, and the area around the strike was sealed off (**forced proximity**) and it became the Shimmer.

Lena's **scar** is her lonely childhood (**orphan**, **fairy tale**). She finds her solace in being alone as a biologist (**profession**).

Lena's **husband**, (**protector**) Kane was a member of the most recent research team who entered the Shimmer. Later, Kane returns as the only survivor (**kidnapped**) who **returned home**. However, Lena realizes that he is not her husband (**twins**, **fake relationship**, **mistaken**

identity). A secret government branch (**antagonist**) whisks Kane away for testing. Guilt over Lena's affair (**love triangle**) and unable to love her husband to the extent he wants (**unrequited love**) motivates Lena to apply for the next Shimmer expedition team (**quest**).

The **Shimmer's** psychologist leader (**antagonist, boss, guardian**) hypnotizes (**amnesia, red herring**) the four female team members (**professions**) so that they may cross the border safely (**quest/journey**). When they regain consciousness, three days have passed (**red herring, time travel**) and the team is deep in the Shimmer.

Inside the Shimmer none of their equipment works (**fish out of water**). Being inside the Shimmer causes mutations in the life forms within its boundaries (**red herring, ugly duckling**). The crew members' corpses from previous expeditions are **victims** of the Shimmer. The **ticking time bomb** is getting out of The Shimmer alive—or unchanged.

The psychologist team leader (**protector**) is keeping **secrets** from the other team members (**fake relationship**) such as she is dying from cancer. She has no intention of taking them back across the border (**red herring**) and without her help the other team members are **stranded**.

Everyone but Lena dies (**victims, violence**) or transforms (**ugly duckling**) into a life form that is different than their pre-Shimmer bodies. Lena feels like she's been inside the Shimmer before (**return to her hometown**).

Reunion with her original husband in The Shimmer is her goal. But in the end, a changeling Lena reunites with her impostor husband.

How is the **suspect trope** used in *Annihilation*: Because of all the **secrets** among everyone involved at every level in The Shimmer, there is a high degree of mistrust among the scientists. This fuels the **conflict** and sense of unreality as there are no allies in the field. **Violence** and **victims** are natural tropes to work with **suspects** as are **antagonists** and **secrets**.

Time Travel

Army of Darkness (1992)

It doesn't matter where or when; it's still about relationships.

Trope Synopsis *Army of Darkness*:

Ash (**protector**, **tortured hero**) **time travels** back to the Middle Ages (**fairy tale**, **fish out of water**), accidentally. He lands (**stranded**) in a war (**secrets**, **scars**, **violence**) between Lord Arthur and Duke Henry (**across the tracks**, **bosses**). Thrown into prison (**forced proximity**, **mistaken identity**), Ash proves his fighting prowess (**ugly duckling**) and is released (**military**, **professions**, **politics**).

Wise Knights (**mentors**) send him on a **quest** for a magic book (**MacGuffin**) with the spells to **return home**.

Ash **road trips** to the book's rumored location where he encounters conflict, such as forgetting the exact magic spell words (**amnesia**) and thinking he slayed his **twin** (**hidden identity**, **red herring**).

His **twin** (**antagonist**) unites the undead into the Army of Darkness which Ash must defeat and rescue Shelia (**family**, **woman in peril**, **unrequited love**), **kidnapped** by the undead.

Ash utters the magic words (**second chance**), **returning to his hometown** timeline. Again, he forgets some words (**amnesia**), and an undead **suspect** sneaks (**stalks**) into the present time without Ash's knowledge (**secret**, **ticking time bomb**). Back at work with his colleagues (**reunion**), the undead **antagonist** from the past attacks Ash (**red herring**, **revenge**, **violence**). Ash kills him (**redemption**).

How the **time travel trope** is used in *Army of Darkness:* It provides a way for a popular character, Ash to have **adventures** outside the normal present-day story setting. It is used like the **amnesia** trope and often used in a series to step outside the story.

Tortured Hero/Heroine

Little Shop of Horrors (1986)

Nice things are not allowed.

Trope Synopsis *Little Shop of Horrors*:

Antagonist Audrey II is a carnivorous plant Seymour (**loner**, **protector**, **tortured hero**) obtained at a mysterious show (**secrets**). Seymour and Audrey (**professionals**) work at an unsuccessful plant store (**workplace**, **forced proximity**). When Audrey suggests Seymour (**guardian**) exhibit Audrey 2 to help business (**the con**), the **boss** agrees.

Seymour discovers Audrey II needs blood to survive (**fake relationship**, **violence**). Seymour and Audrey are unaware they have **unrequited love** for each other. Audrey's horrible boyfriend (**love triangle**) is a dentist (**profession**).

Seymour (**fish out of water**) is unable to keep up with Audrey II's blood feedings; she (**antagonist**) suggests a **victim**. Seymour plans to kill Audrey's boyfriend but he can't go through with it. The dentist accidentally kills himself (**second chance**). Seymour's boss sees him butchering the corpse and he believes Seymour is a murderer (**mistaken identity**). Seymour feeds the corpse to Audrey II who grows a lot (**ugly duckling**).

Seymour's boss **blackmails** him into leaving town. Audrey II (**antagonist**, **stalker**) swallows (**kidnaps**) the **boss** (**victim**) rather than lose Seymour (**unrequited love**).

Seymour and Audrey plan to run away together (**reunion**). Audrey II tries to kill Audrey (**red herring**, **stranded**) to prevent Seymour from leaving her (**revenge**). Seymour saves Audrey from Audrey II (**redemption**).

A businessman wants to breed the Audrey II plant, but Seymour knows it must be destroyed (**quest**). Audrey II is revealed to be a space alien (**hidden identity**) who tries to kill Seymour. He ends up killing Audrey II in self-defense. Audrey and Seymour marry (**family**, **second chance**) and move away from the city (**reunion**).

In their garden, a small Audrey II plant begins to grow (**ticking time bomb**).

How the **tortured hero/heroine** trope is used in *Little Shop of Horrors:* Seymour is at the mercy of a carnivorous plant, so it is a key aspect of his character. The **tortured**

hero/heroine is a horror staple because we need horrible events to happen to them for **conflict**. If a character isn't suffering some kind of mental or physical torture, then we aren't able to increase their misery. And if it's one thing we all know from storytelling, it's that things can always get worse. This is a trope that works with other trope types very easily.

Twins

The Shinning (1980)

Two are better than one.

Trope Synopsis *The Shinning*:

Writer Jack (**antagonist**, **profession**) takes a job as a winter caretaker (**domestic staff**, **loner**) at a closed resort (**forced proximity**) to work on his book (**quest**). His wife and son (**family**) join him. His young son has developed supernatural powers (**secrets**, **ticking time bomb**, **ugly duckling**). Ghosts (**antagonists**, **hidden identities**, **victims**) at the hotel **stalk** Jack and his family (**fish out of water**).

Jack learns a former caretaker killed his family and himself (**fairy tale**, **secrets**, **ticking time bomb**, **violence**) in the hotel. **Twin** girl ghosts harm Jack's son (**stranded**) but Jack blames him (**mistaken identity**). Jack's mental health continues to decline (**tortured hero**) as ghosts (**antagonists**) **stalk** him. Jack's wife realizes Jack is having **violent** and paranoid thoughts (**fake relationship**, **stranded**). Jack attacks his wife and son (**scars**, **violence**). Both escape temporarily (**second chance**). Jack's son sends a telepathic message to a friend for help (**best friend**). The friend arrives and distracts Jack (**red herring**) so the wife and son can escape in the friend's vehicle (**return to hometown**, **reunion**, **road trip**). Jack kills the friend (**revenge**) and then dies. Jack's image appears in a hotel picture from before his birth (**secrets**, **suspects**).

How the **twin trope** is used in *The Shinning*: The use of **twins** provides a way for those around us (in **family** ties and geography) to have **hidden identities** as **antagonists** without suspicion. The **twin trope** in horror, whether it is having an Other Mother in *Coraline,* **siblings** in *The Witch,* or the ghost twins in *The Shinning* are intended to confuse and threaten the **protagonist**.

Unrequited love

What Lies Beneath (2000)

Love, like life, is unequal.

Trope Synopsis *What Lies Beneath*:

A married couple (**forced proximity**), Claire and Norman (**family**, **professions**), **suspect** their new neighbors have a **violent** relationship (**red herring**). When the wife goes missing (**road trip**, **victim**), Claire thinks she sees her body (**mistaken identity**, **red herring**) in lake next door (**forced proximity**). Claire and **her best friend** hold a séance (**quest**) where the missing woman's initials appear on a mirror (**secrets**).

The neighbor reappears unharmed (**reunion**). Norman belittles Claire (**unrequited love**) over her theory. Claire discovers that her husband (**boss**) had an affair (**age difference**, **fake relationship**, **workplace**) with a now-deceased student (**scar**, **victim**) having the same initials (**red herring**) as her neighbor (**ticking time bomb**).

Claire investigates the death (**quest**) and finds some of her possessions (**MacGuffin**). Claire calls the dead woman's spirit forth and while possessed (**fish out of water**, **kidnapped**) she seduces Norman (**mistaken identity**). He realizes that his dead lover (**hidden identity**) is haunting (**stalking**) him from beyond the grave (**suspect**, **unrequited love**). Claire (**tortured heroine**) remembers (**amnesia**) that Norman had an affair with a student (**tortured heroine, victim**).

Claire finds Norman almost drowned in the bathtub (**victim**) where he refutes killing the student or trying to kill himself (**red herring**, **secrets**).

Claire is drawn to the lake water and almost drowns (**stranded**). Norman saves her (**protector**). Claire discovers more possessions of the dead student in the lake (**MacGuffin**). Norman says the student killed herself in their house and he dumped her body and car in the lake (**fake relationship**). He promises to turn himself in to the police but lies (**the con**). He tries to kill Claire (**woman in peril**), telling her he (**antagonist**) did kill (**violence**) the student (**victim**) because she was **blackmailing** him (**boss**, **politics**). The dead woman's ghost possesses Claire's body scaring Norman (**stalker**). Claire saves herself (**guardian**) and then escapes in their truck. Norman is hidden in the back and tries to kill her again (**stranded**, **woman in peril**). The ghost saves Claire as Norman drowns in the lake (**revenge**). Claire (**scars**, **widow**) visits the dead student's grave with flowers (**redemption**).

How the **unrequited love trope** works in *What Lies Beneath*: For much of this story, the **woman in peril trope** supports **unrequited love**. Claire and the student her husband killed are both harmed by Norman. But he is not revealed to be more than a **red herring** and **victim** until much later in the story. The question of affection and the power that is associated with it are intertwined in this story. All kinds of **secrets** also work well with the **unrequited love trope**.

Victims

World War Z (2013)

No one wants to be one.

Trope Synopsis *World War Z*:

Gerry is a UN inspector who is trying to keep his **family** safe (**protector**, **quest**) during a zombie outbreak (**antagonists**, **violence**). His **boss blackmails** him to find patient zero (**MacGuffin**) of the outbreak in order to keep his family and an **orphan** safe on a ship (**forced proximity**). Anyone bitten by a zombie becomes an **antagonist**, **ugly duckling**, **and victim**.

Gerry (**loner**, **tortured hero**) **road trips** to various international locations. Meanwhile, zombie hoards overrun cities around the globe (**stalking**, **stranded**). Gerry discovers it takes twelve seconds to become infected after a bite (**ticking time bomb**). He also discovers a physician (**antagonist**, **politics**, **secrets**, **suspect**) released the virus.

When one of Gerry's colleagues is bitten (**woman in peril**), he amputates her hand to save her life (**scar, second chance, violence**). Gerry notices zombies ignore sick humans (**hidden identity/disguise**). He theorizes that is because the zombies want healthy hosts to spread the disease (**bet/wager**). When he's **stranded** amongst a zombie hoard in a lab, he injects himself with the pathogen. His plan works (**the con**); the zombies ignore him (**redemption**).

How the **victim trope** is used in *World War Z*: It functions as a **MacGuffin** in this story because the **victims** are also **suspects**. He tries to prevent the **ugly duckling** transformation from happening in the first place. The story is a straight-up **quest** story, so the **conflict** comes from threats to relationships which means **antagonist**, **forced proximity**, **secrets**, and **ticking time bomb** work well with **victims**.

PART TWO

Ok, so now that we looked at thirty-plus common tropes in horror, we have our feet wet trope wise. Let's look at the dozen (or dozens?) that are pretty much in every horror plot. Remember the quote from Blake's *Save The Cat* about the studio exec calling for *give me the same, but different*?

What *is* the same but different? Tropes.

We're looking for new ways to combine these building blocks. We're searching for relationships that can thrill us by taking us deep into a character's private fears.

To do that, we're going to compare and contrast some of the same examples we talked about in Part I with Horror Trope big guns now.

An important thing to remember about tropes is that they are used to varying degrees in our creations; we don't give them all equal time and love. Use 'em where and how you need them in detail to create multilayered characters.

Antagonist/Villain

How the antagonist trope is used in horror:

The **antagonist** is the driving force in a gripping horror story.

But why?

Because the **antagonist** forces the protagonist to bring their A-game to the match.

In horror, **antagonists** come in all forms which is a key part of the delight in this genre. Let's take a look.

In the Horror genre, everybody expects to find **antagonists** like zombies. They're (usually) easy to spot. They're the **antagonists** in *Army of the Dead, Kingdom, Pride and Prejudice and Zombies, Zombieland,* and *World War Z.*

These **antagonists** are identifiable. The threat they pose is lethal; avoiding close physical contact is pretty much the goal. But because we need conflict we're getting the antagonist-protagonist band together. Here are some tropes we can use to battle the monsters we know: **forced proximity, road trip, and quest**.

Now think about another kind of **antagonist**. One who is more sophisticated than a brutish brain-eating hoard but still a known quantity. Hannibal Lecter is a serial killer serving life imprisonment behind some very thick plexiglass in *Silence of the Lambs*. Lecter acts as Clarice's **mentor**, pushing her to track a serial killer. It's a traumatic experience for her but she does get the outcome she desired.

It's all well and good to go raging off to battle monsters that we know about. But life is usually more complicated than that.

What about the monsters we can't see?

That's a pretty big crowd when we stop to think about it.

We have **Unseen Antagonists** who are strangers like in *Alien, Predator, and Candyman* that are **stalking** their **victims** with **forced proximity**. Those are pretty creepy.

But my favorite category of **Unseen Antagonists** is the ones who already have a relationship with the **victims**—their family and friends. They are the ones that the protagonist, and usually the audience, least **suspect**.

Why are these my favorites? Because those **antagonists** are the ones that can do the most damage by being so close to the protagonist. They know the protagonist's vulnerabilities and they are happy to exploit them. They are hidden functions like **red herrings**, diverting our attention from their possibility of betrayal.

Let's look at some examples in increasing circles of intimacy.

We'll start with the neighbors as **antagonists** in *The Purge.* They come to the family's rescue while they are under a mob attack only to reveal that they plan to kill the family themselves. What a delicious reveal in the story! The widowed mother realizes the enemy is within her house. It's fantastic story tension.

Or what about the protagonist, Sidney, in *Scream*? She unknowingly gives her virginity to the guy who killed her mother and plans to kill her and her father also. The betrayal at finding out the **antagonist** is someone she trusted all along.

In *The Invisible Man,* the protagonist discovers she's in an abusive relationship. Her attempts to get free of him are thwarted at every turn because he knows her so well (plus he has the advantage of being invisible).

The **antagonist** stalks the family from within in *The Omen* with Damian as the devil's spawn. In both these cases, the **antagonist** is living within the family as it stalks them.

And finally, think about the **antagonist** as part of oneself. In *Psycho,* Norman Bates has killed his mother, yet he can't accept that. He *is* the **antagonist**.

How deliciously creepy is that! They aren't even aware of the threat within their seemingly safe relationships—their guard is down, and the killer is literally within reach.

The **antagonist** trope can be used with any other tropes, but here a few to get started: **hidden identity**, **mistaken identity**, **fake relationship**, **suspect**, **victims**, **and violence**. Combine them to make it even more powerful and drive our dear protagonists to their breaking point.

Disguise/Hidden Identity

There are so many uses for the **hidden identity trope** because this trope has a **secret** embedded in it. It's one of those twofers I love (like #secretbaby). It is a trope that is powered by character developing a relationship that is based on a lie. That, my friends, is storytelling gold.

Sometimes we're in such a rush to keep our stories moving, that we forget that it's important to make sure we don't rush the reveal.

This trope has (1) a reason for the **secret**, (2) someone/something who wants to maintain the secret, (3) the effect(s) on the protagonist who is being kept in the dark, (4) and choosing the worst possible time for the reveal to the protagonist.

For example, in *Scream,* the **antagonists** are two guys sharing a masked identity. Even though Sidney occasionally has suspicions, her boyfriend has an alibi. When is the worst time for a **hidden identity** reveal? When the character is at their most vulnerable. It's a painful but effective plot point—Sidney gives her virginity to the boyfriend (her most vulnerable point) only to discover immediately afterward that he killed her mother last year out of **revenge**, plans to kill Sidney and her father, and make it look like a murder-suicide.

The **hidden identity trope** has been combined with **antagonist**, **jealousy**, **kidnapping**, **red herring**, **revenge**, **secrets**, **suspects**, **victim**, and **woman in peril**.

In *Saw*, the **hidden identity** is Jigsaw, the killer. At the beginning of the movie, he's the unidentified **victim** (& supposed corpse) lying on the floor in the bathroom with the two kidnapping **victims**. He's privy to all the conversations between the two **victims**, watching their decision-making unfold. His reveal is at the story's end when he leaves his **victim** behind. The tropes combined with **hidden identity** in *Scream* include **antagonist**, **boss**, **fake relationship**, **suspects**, and **victim**.

What We Do in the Shadows (WWDIS) Season One has a twist on the **hidden identity trope**. Guillermo, the vampire's human familiar and hopeful vampire, discovers his **hidden identity** is a **secret heir**; he has Van Helsing, vampire killer, DNA. Naturally, he can't tell his bungling vampire employers, but he also won't allow them to be murdered by the **revenge**-seeking vampires **stalking** them. His solution is to become their **secret protector**, eliminating all the threats that come to kill them without them being any the wiser that they are in danger.

The tropes combined with WWDIS and **hidden identity** are **antagonist**, **protector**, **red herring**, **suspects**, **victim**, and **violence**. Let the reveal unfold and raise the stakes of discovery as the story develops.

Forced Proximity

Forced proximity is the locked room concept that we often see in mysteries. Confined space is pretty much a given in the horror genre.

Why? Because it means assured **conflict** when there's nowhere to run. It keeps the story tension high. We want that. We don't want protagonists that can get plenty of sleep, food, and emotional support, not to mention weapons. We want them at their wits' end.

For example, let's think about how the two men chained up in *Saw's* gross bathroom works the **forced proximity trope**. It sets up the rest of the story. There are plenty of tropes packed effectively into *Saw* but **forced proximity** is what makes it unique when combined with the life-or-death question.

However clever the original Saw was though; we can't all write stories set in a nasty bathroom. And that's not the end of the good news. Let's look at how we can use **forced proximity** in a range of physical spaces.

In *The Purge*, the whole story is set within the confines of a house/yard during a city-wide lockdown. It turns out that the home's exterior is more porous than previously thought, yielding an influx of new raiders. But the story's focus remains inside the house.

Kingdom calls out the **forced proximity trope** in its title. A zombie plague has infected part of the land, and the **antagonists** want to spread the plague. The prince's subjects seek to contain and eradicate it. Challenges in a larger space include fire, fog, hunger, and illness. And then there's the scene with all the top bureaucrats escaping on a ship to save themselves, leaving the people to face the zombies at nightfall alone. Only one grieving mother has brought her zombie son along in a locked chest. Once she opens it the ship is **forced into proximity** to be with a hungry zombie and his **victims**.

Alien shows us that space is a vacuum with a limited number of good places to survive. Ripley's crew finds themselves trapped on their ship with a deadly alien **stalking** them as they journey back to earth. As the story progresses, Ripley's options to escape the alien grow more restricted. At last, she's left facing off against the alien in an escape pod.

In *Raised by Wolves,* one rocky planet with a breathable atmosphere isn't big enough for the two former earth enemies. As the first settlers, the atheists have the first claim but when the Mithraics' spaceship crashes, they wind up sharing space. And it does not go well.

Forced proximity doesn't only have to be a fixed location; it only needs to be confined. *Zombieland* uses vehicles as **forced proximity** when the only survivors of the apocalypse band together to drive across the country (**road trip**).

There are other tropes besides **road trip** that works well in **forced proximity**. Here are five:

In *Bird Box*, Malorie and the kids are blindfolded (**fish out of water**) in a rowboat (**forced proximity**) rowing down a river (**quest**).

In Little Shop of Horrors, Audrey is **kidnapped** by Audrey II in the plant shop (**forced proximity**) to eat her.

The Invisible Man twists her billionaire boyfriend's domestic abuse at home (**forced proximity**). Her **revenge** is when she dons the invisible suit, kills him, and makes it look like suicide.

When Leah, in *Annihilation,* crosses the border into The Shimmer (**forced proximity**) she is **stranded** because she needs hypnosis to get back over the border.

In *Silence of the Lambs,* Claire meets with Hannibal Lecter in his prison (**forced proximity**) to catch (**quest**) another serial killer.

MacGuffin

A MacGuffin is a lost physical object. It's popular with any story that involves a question or **quest**.

The **MacGuffin** works with so many other tropes but a few like **antagonist**, **red herring**, **forced proximity**, and **hidden identity** all fold into using the **MacGuffin** pretty easily.

Let's look at some **MacGuffins** in the following examples:

Saw (key)

Silence of the Lambs (buffalo bill)

Midsommar (ritual book)

Alien (alien)

The Invisible Man (invisible suit)

What Lies Beneath (locket)

Army of the Dead (treasure/zombie queen head)

Kingdom (plant causing the disease)

The feeding frenzy created by multiple parties wanting the object creates wonderful relationship **conflict**. We see scenes where the protagonist is pushed beyond their limits and forced to sacrifice what they hold most dear.

Politics

Politics in tropes has nothing to do with what we see in the news. I'm talking about the dynamics of relationships in the worlds we build.

Like the **antagonist** trope, **politics** can be combined with any number of other tropes to deepen worldbuilding. That is crucial to keeping our audience in the story.

Carrie reminded us of the **politics** of high school, the power of popularity, the desire to be included, and the loneliness of being on the outside. When combined with tropes like **revenge**, **forced proximity**, **hidden identity**, **ticking time bomb**, and **violence** it fueled an explosive story.

Anytime there are two or more characters there's going to be **politics**. The greater the group, the more potential **conflict**.

Beyond *Carrie,* there are many examples of **politics** in other hostile communities besides high school. In *The*

Witch, the family is banished from their community and at the mercy of sinister woods that pits the **family** members against each other.

In *Raised by Wolves,* one planet isn't large enough for two groups of settlers where safety and starvation are daily challenges. **Military** communities like ship crew members in *Alien* or bands of mercenaries *in Predator* and *Army of the Dead,* all have to navigate group dynamics to survive.

Politics is a pretty powerful trope when it's tied into a question of survival.

Let's talk about **politics** in workplace dynamics. Whether you've done a group project recently or not, the same character tropes pop up: the **boss**, the **chatty one** who does little but talk, the **worrier** who needs constant reassurance, the **maverick**, and the **quiet worker bee**.

In *Severance*, the **politics** of working on a severed floor for the Lumen Corp means basic life in prison. The workers in Data Refinement are actively discouraged from communicating with other Lumen employees. When the department violates that directive, the consequences cause a complete unraveling of the status quo.

And the **politics** of the department are forever changed by the introduction of a new group member, Helly R. She is the most rebellious of new employees and she disrupts the routine of the MDR department with her repeated escape attempts. Later, when she learns she is a

secret heir to the Lumen Corp, the irony of her dislike for being severed is delicious.

Don't forget **politics** closer to home though, too. Any **family** that has more than two members experiences alliances.

Think about neighborhood group dynamics in *The Purge*. During an attack, the **family** learns that their neighbors aren't there to support them; they showed up to kill them. And yet, the family chooses to remain living with neighbors who hate them so much instead of giving them the satisfaction of moving away.

In *The Omen* and *Psycho,* both of those stories involve **politics** within the **family**. In *The Omen*, Damian is actively pushing to destroy the **family** by manipulating his parents with the help of his nanny. In *Psycho*, Norman Bates assumes his dead mother's persona. He so thoroughly occupies that place that everyone overhearing their arguments assumes that she is alive until the end of the story.

Time to get down and dirty with **politics** in your own work? **Family** dynamics? Work? Friendships? Push back the fear of getting it wrong. Instead, focus on going deeper in your story.

Protector/Warrior

When a story has an **antagonist**, there's always going to be someone or something to push back against their dastardly planning.

That someone is most often the **protector** or **warrior** type. It's easy to think of **warriors** as Ripley in *Alien*, or as the mercenaries in *Army of the Dead* or *Predator*. These are soldiers who are trained to protect though maybe not ready initially for what they are up against. In the end, they come through.

But what about **protectors** that aren't quite so obvious? *Pride and Prejudice and Zombies* features young gentlewomen trained in the martial art of zombie defense. That is an unexpected twist on the **protector trope** along with **hidden identity**, **red herring**, **revenge**, **secrets**, and **ticking time bomb**, just to name a few.

In *Annihilation*, the soldier, Lena, is a former biologist. She comes to the Shimmer searching for answers about what happened to her husband. She is seeking to protect herself and the others but once inside, it becomes clear that life in the Shimmer is nothing she'd experienced before.

Now we come to my favorite group, the **unlikely warriors**. These aren't characters with training or uniforms. Weapons aren't necessarily a given.

But what they lack in official qualifications, they make up for in courage.

Let's think about Shaun's character in *Shaun of the Dead;* he's a beleaguered salesman who isn't respected by his coworkers and stepfather. Shaun avoids life by gaming with his **best friend** until his girlfriend breaks up with him. And the zombie apocalypse arrives.

Now Shaun is saving those he loves—his girlfriend, mother, and **best friend** by fighting off zombies. His transformation into a **warrior** uses the **ugly duckling trope** and **fish out of water** in his **quest**.

Guillermo in *What We Do in the Shadows* is another example of an **unexpected warrior**. He's the comfortable-looking **domestic servant**/familiar of a powerful vampire, but Guillermo saves his clueless **boss** regularly. And then there's *Zombieland's* Columbus who was an awkward college student (with a fear of clowns) that ends up being a successful **warrior** against zombies.

But it's the **women warriors** who shine in the horror genre.

Mothers as **protectors** is a common trope. There's pregnant Evelyn from *The Quiet Place* who battles the Death Angels **stalking** her family. Rosemary in *Rosemary's Baby* endures a horrible pregnancy and then gives birth to a demon, but she still wants to protect him. In *Cujo*, the mother risks her life repeatedly to fight a rabid dog to protect her son.

Even in *Psycho*, Norman Bates acts out his mother protecting him even though that's a situation gone very wrong.

Then there are the young women facing off as warriors with more experience with **antagonists** like Thomasin in *The Witch*, Clarice in *Silence of the Lamb*s, and Sidney in *Scream.*

Finally, kids are **warriors** in horror too like Coraline who battles an evil replica of her mother. There's also the little Finnish boy in *Rare Exports* who fights a Christmas demon.

The **Protector** trope works with so many tropes.

Are you getting ideas about how **protector tropes** can play into your next project? What other tropes can you string together to create a protagonist that has many sides to their character?

Red Herring

The **red herring trope** is all about the tension of misdirection.

It's the equivalent of a magician saying, "Look here, there's nothing up my sleeve," while their other hand is palming the quarter that they will pull from some assistant's ear later.

We want that level of audience trust in our stories to pull them, making them follow us without question.

Why?

Because later, when we reveal the misstep, the surprise is that much greater for the audience. That gap we have created is story tension.

Before we take a look at a few movie/series examples, here's my shameless plug for American Goddess/Grandmother of American Horror, Shirley Jackson.

I read her short story, "The Lottery", as a high school student many eons ago. In the story, set in a small community, the members gather for a lottery. The young narrator's hopes to select the winning ticket build throughout the story as the community gathers. All she knows is the winner selects a piece of paper from the pile that is distinctive. Her anticipation builds until her turn. She opens her ticket to find it has a black spot on it. She has won! Her elation at being chosen and feeling special courses through her. Until she wonders what she has won and that coincides with her community each picking up a rock and stoning her to death.

When I finished it, I was deeply shocked—I didn't know you could do that in a story. It was the first time I was ever aware of misdirection in a story. Jackson took something we generally associate as positive—a lottery and a small community. And she flips that assumption right over into betrayal.

Jackson does what we all want to experience with a **red herring**; it's that snap where suddenly your perspective in the story becomes just a little tighter and you see the truth.

That's a hell of a ride.

Jackson's two novellas, *The Haunting of Hill House* and *We Have Always Lived in a Castle* (my personal favorite) are excellent examples of misdirection in written stories that are worth a study.

But back to our examples!

Red herrings can be persons, places, or objects. And the most compelling stories use all three.

There's no need to be sparing with **red herrings**! Use them as often as you like. The key is tying them back to the story.

In *Saw*, a hospital orderly, Zep is a **red herring**. We first meet Zep through a flashback with one of the main characters, Doctor Gordon who is presently chained up in the bathroom. We are introduced to him as a hospital orderly, someone non-threatening is our first impression. Later, Gordon recognizes Zep in a box of pictures found in their prison. Ok, now we know he's not just an orderly he's up to something. But what?

Then we learn Zep is holding Gordon's family hostage. When his family escapes, Zep comes looking for Gordon. By now, the audience and the prisoners are sure Zep is Jigsaw. Then he reveals he's also caught up in Jigsaw's games as a player, not the mastermind. Zep dies and the game isn't over. Now what? In our collective audience shock (as well as the unfortunate bathroom victims), we are scrambling to figure out what the hell just happened. If the culprit isn't Zep, who can it be? Desperate times and all that as Gordon cuts his foot off to escape. Now Adam is left alone, with two corpses, Zep and the unidentified guy—who we learn isn't dead after all and is Jigsaw. That's some seriously good misdirection.

In *Kingdom*, the prince's loyal band of rebels assumes that because the zombies have previously attacked only at night, they are active by the lack of sun.

However, the **antagonistic** chief councilor waits in hiding, watching for the rebels' miscalculation. As they pack their fortifications away, the zombies attack at sunrise.

What?!

The prince realizes the truth, it's the cold that activates them, not the light. Misdirection strikes again!

In *Rare Exports,* the concept that a present-day beloved Christmas icon shares the same origin as the unearthed demonic deity is a series of **red herrings**. Since the main character is a child, the fact that no one takes his concerns or observations seriously until critical points in the story only reinforce the reveal that the demons are real. Children are discounted by adults all the time. See how the misdirection worked here? Disregard the young at our peril.

Scar

The **scar trope** is often called a character's wound. Its story purpose is to give them an enriched backstory by an important past event. A **scar** can be whatever works in that character's world.

It can be being bullied like in *Carrie,* or it can be like Tallahassee losing his son in *Zombieland.* It needs to be meaningful to the character and something they can't move ahead in life without carrying it with them. Sometimes it gets resolved on a positive note as in Tallahassee adopting his new **road trip family** in the zombie apocalypse. Sometimes there's no growth involved but chaos and carnage as in *Carrie*. A **scar** can be private information or well-known but as a past event it informs their current decision-making.

Secret

The **secret** can be a past or present-day trope. Its value is that the character is vested in keeping the contents private. It's ripe material to use with the **blackmail trope**. There are similarities to the **scar trope** in that the **secret** has to be meaningful to the character. In thinking about *Carrie* again, her recent development of telekinesis powers is a huge **secret**. She's already marked as a freak by the school bullies, but that ability sets her apart even more. No wonder she conceals it until she can't contain herself anymore.

Secrets are time sensitive in story building. If there is a **secret** that doesn't impact the story, then it's not much of a **conflict**. We want **secrets** that add to the tension, make our characters choose paths under pressure and then go to any lengths to prevent exposure.

This trope is the Labrador Retriever of tropes; it plays well with everything. It pairs especially easy with **antago-**

nist, **hidden identity**, **mistaken identity**, **red herring**, and **ticking time bomb**.

Ticking Time Bomb (TTB)

The time-sensitive goal is a storytelling gift. It gives us an external deadline to ramp up the tension our characters are dealing with.

Without a time limit, stories can drag out which we want to avoid at all costs. Drawn-out stories remind me there's laundry to do. And I hate laundry. I want a story that keeps me riveted because there's only a certain length of time this problem can be solved.

Important elements to remember about **TTB**; the protagonist needs to be aware of the deadline, and there should be story **conflict** that indicates events are getting harder for them to meet that goal. And close to the **TTB** release, it should seem like the protagonist can't possibly succeed. We as storytellers decide whether when **TTB** goes off, it's a success or failure for the protagonist.

Before we look at some examples of the **ticking time bomb (TTB) trope** in action, let's look at what other tropes play well with **TTB**: **forced proximity**, **heist**, **hidden identity**, **quest**, **road trip**, **secret baby**, and **ugly duckling**. It can work with pretty much any other trope but those above are a good starting place if you are just starting to give this trope a try.

In some stories, the **ticking time bomb** is easy to spot. In *Predator,* the protagonist fights the alien, trying to defeat it and make it back to his extraction point. He only has a limited amount of time to get there; the helicopter isn't waiting for him. That's an obvious **ticking time bomb** and it suits the story just fine.

In *Pride and Prejudice and Zombies*, the **hidden identity trope** works with **TTB**. Wickham has been bitten by a zombie, but his transformation is delayed by animal blood and brains. In the meantime, he courted Lizzy and then ran off with her foolish sister, Lydia. Darcy gets her back from Wickham before the family reputation is ruined and she is harmed.

TTB is a natural ally with the **forced proximity trope**. In *Army of the Dead, Carrie, Midsommar, The Purge,* and *The Shining,* the **TTB** is some kind of event. The whole story leads up to what will be the outcome of the **heist**, prom, festival, purge, and end of winter.

TTB and the **ugly duckling trope** give us a time-sensitive date for a transformation. Cujo's rabies and Carrie's Prom are two such examples. The metamorphosis of the scientist into a human fly hybrid uses these two tropes plus a **hidden identity**, **love triangle**, **revenge**, and **violence**. The caretaker's descent into madness in The

Shinning provides another example of a complete transformation in a closed resort during winter (**forced proximity, TTB**).

Does this get your brain firing away on different events you can create to ramp up pressure in your story?

Ugly Duckling

The origins of this trope are the ugly duckling turning into a swan. Since I don't find ducklings ugly, I always feel like the name trivializes this trope's power.

This is a **change** or **transformation trope** that is a staple of the horror genre. The changes a character undergoes is the heart of the story because it impacts relationships.

What tropes work well with **ugly duckling**: **best friend**, **family**, **forced proximity**, **fish out of water**, **hidden identity**, **loner**, **revenge**, **secrets**, **stalker**, **suspect**, **unrequited love**, **victim**, and **violence**.

Notice that the **transformation** is very personal both to the character undergoing the process and those involved in close relationships with them.

Man's **best friend** becomes a rabid beast? *Cujo*.

Think about how different the tension would be if Cujo was a rabid stray dog instead a beloved pet of his **best friend**. It wouldn't be nearly as tense. Why? Because trusting the **transformation** of character before they begin their change makes them becoming something monstrous that much more threatening.

In *Carrie*, a terrible prank startles the **tortured heroine** into releasing her telekinetic powers where she becomes a monster. It results in many **victims** dying at the high school. Eventually, she kills her tormentors (school bullies and her mother), but she chooses death for herself in the end.

Let's look at another example; in *The Shinning,* a father takes a **caretaker** job at an isolated resort to provide for his **family** only to suffer a murderous mental breakdown and try to kill them. Having it be the father **transforming** into a murderous beast intent on killing his own family is packed with more **conflict** than if he was killing random **victims**. And tied into that, if the mother and son being **stalked** by an unknown person provides much less tension than it being a husband/father.

Now that we have that idea in our heads, let's look at some examples of the **ugly duckling trope** that focus on physical and mental **transformations**.

In *The Fly,* the scientist undergoes mental and physical mutations to become a human-fly hybrid.

The tortured, tolerated heroine Dani in *Midsommar* spends most of her time crying and feeling lost, and

transforms into a literal queen at the festival ritual who orders the murder of her cheating boyfriend.

Other **ugly transformations** don't require a physical change but rather a mental one.

In *Coraline*, our heroine comes to understand that the love The Other Mother offers is false while what her parents give her is true.

Thomasin in *The Witch* loses her family to the dark powers living in the woods. She's falsely accused of witchcraft and watches her family members die. After she kills her mother in self-defense, she chooses to join the witches instead of being alone.

Ok, what kind of transformation tropes can you think of? Make a list, it doesn't have to be in horror. It can be anything that challenges the protagonists' identity. Bonus points though if a monster is involved.

Woman in Peril/ Protagonist in Peril

Before I started this book, I didn't realize how popular the **woman in peril trope** was in the horror genre. Sure, I'd seen clips of Psycho's shower scene used for horror marketing, but it never dawned on me just how central that trope was to horror until this project.

Now it makes sense though since horror is the study of monsters, "it's all women and children first" as the prey. Looking back at *Psycho*'s shower scene, Marion as the lone woman thief who happens into Norman Bates' motel is the perfect **victim**.

Not surprisingly there are many examples of women and children as **victims** in horror: Damian's mother and unborn child in *The Omen,* the children in *Rare Exports*, villagers in *Kingdom*, Thomasin's **family** in *The Witch,* and the husband's young student lover in *What Lies Beneath*.

But what I love about the **woman in peril trope** is that it's as much about the twist of women becoming **survivors, protectors**, and even a few **suspects**.

Here are a few other tropes that work well with **woman in peril**: **across the tracks**, **boss**, **the con**, **fake relationship**, **family**, **forced proximity**, **hidden identity**, **protector**, **revenge**, **reunion**, **second chance**, **secrets**, **stranded**, **suspects**, **ticking time bomb**, **ugly duckling**, **unrequited love**, **victim**, **violence**.

There's a great combination I've noticed with the **women in peril trope** that I admire that moves beyond just the **victim**. That is adding the **ugly duckling** as the **transformation trope** plus the **protector trope**.

This is exciting stuff! Let's take a look at some examples.

In *Cujo*, the mother takes on the rabid monster after the deaths of two men and succeeds in killing Cujo.

In *The Quiet Place*, Evelyn the mother manages to safely deliver her baby and vanquish the death angels. Her daughter discovers her hearing aid at an awkward pitch can repel the death angels and uses this knowledge as a weapon to save the family.

In *The Invisible Man,* Cecilia escapes her abusive lover only to be framed for her sister's murder by him. She counters this by faking her death, escaping prison, and using a second stolen invisible skin suit to take **revenge** on him. Eventually, she kills him wearing the invisible suit with an airtight alibi so that she can be free.

In *The Purge,* the mother becomes a **widow** as her neighbors seemingly come to the family's rescue. Only she learns that they are not allies but have come to kill her **family** out of **revenge** and **jealousy**. Even with them in her house during the lockdown, she fights to defend her **family**. She and her children survive The Purge.

Finally, in *What Lies Beneath,* Claire investigates her husband's past affair with a student. In the process, Claire discovers her husband is a murderer and the **victim's** ghost seeks **revenge**. Claire escapes her husband's attempts to murder her to keep the past hidden. The ghost saves Claire's life, gets **revenge** on her killer, and finally finds peace with Claire's help.

Summary

I hope that these twelve tropes have shown how you can use them as a base to build some pretty complex characters. These twelve are not the only trope superheroes. Maybe you see five or twenty tropes as the basis for your story. That is fine! It's a subjective process. And with tropes I generally think the more, the merrier.

Let this be a jumping off point for how you use tropes to make connections because those connections pull the story world tighter. Writing this book has really inspired me to think about how to create new stories after I've studied all the ways others have been formed.

Whatever is on your top trope hot list though, leave a space for one more. We aren't done yet! I've saved my favorite trope for last because I wanted us to be armed with as much knowledge as possible as we go forth.

Are you ready to take a step into that most mysterious of tropes?

Dare I say, it's unforgettable?

That's right, peeps, I'm talking the amnesia trope.

Part Three

The Amnesia Trope

More than a Knock on the Head

Truth time.

I don't just love the **amnesia trope** (aka the loss of memories); I'm obsessed with it.

All our talk about tropes and their relationships in Part I and II has been leading us up to this chapter. I wrote this book specifically so I could write about the **amnesia trope**. I'm so stinking excited to talk with you about this, I've let my carbonated beverage get so flat!

I've met many authors who hate using the amnesia trope. And it's certainly not used very often compared to the other big gun tropes.

What's so great about the amnesia trope?

First, we need to realize that everyone has memories. It seems obvious, but until I started working on this chapter it never occurred to me that memories were a potential story building block. Heck, even Leatherface in

Texas Chainsaw Massacre (1974) has memories (plus a serious need for family therapy).

Mostly we see the **amnesia trope** used as a character's temporary (convenient) loss of memory to pause a particular relationship-based plot line. And yes, it usually involves some kind of head injury.

By the way, that's not just in horror but across every other genre too. I've been guilty of employing the head whomp for temporary memory loss in my own stories. And this trope does work well when you set it up with unrequited love.

The head whomp device allows you to advance (or pause) a relationship, giving the audience what they have been craving—then you take it away with a relationship reset when the memories return. It's something we see often in storytelling because it works.

Yet, I look back at my own work and I see so many missed opportunities.

Here's my epiphany: **the amnesia trope can be so much more**.

How?

By mining the connection between relationship and memory.

Simply put, the **amnesia trope** is a story building block with the concept of missing memory (aka a relationship).

Notice how characters with amnesia don't forget how to tie their shoes or use a fork.

Because what are our most powerful memories about? Relationships.

Memories are the product of relationships, but they aren't tangible. We try to hold onto memories with physical things. Think of a favorite childhood toy stored away by an adult. Think of the power of family heirlooms. Think of the storage units everywhere housing massive amounts of memory in the form of old photo albums, gifts, and old sports trophies.

Ok, so memories are part of what makes us human. We can use that emotional connection to suck the audience into our stories.

When we subtract the memories temporarily, it's like an earthquake for our characters. We have just caused massive story instability, which is storytelling gold.

Amnesia is a **quest** trope—find out what was lost. It's a story within a story. But more than being some tangential story line, the **amnesia trope** can reveal layers of the protagonist's character.

So, I want you to reconsider the **amnesia trope** in a new light. And I'm going to show you how this trope can add depth your stories.

To do that we're going to fillet two recent **amnesia trope** examples, the 2017 movie *Get Out* and Apple TV's 2022 series *Severance*.

Example #1

Get Out (2017)

Jordan Peele wrote the script and directed *Get Out.* Honestly, there are days that his level of storytelling genius makes me want to curl into a ball and have a good cry. Luckily there's a greater number of days that I am thankful for Peele's talent.

First, the movie is a great thriller with wonderfully terrible monsters. It's the kind of story anyone can get caught up in. You know what I'm talking about; we all want the experience of having a few hours of relief from our daily life. If we didn't, we wouldn't be storytellers.

But *Get Out* isn't just an escapist diversion; it's a master-class in storytelling structure that we can all learn from. And hopefully, I've convinced you that like me studying the structure of a really great story is not only helpful to our creative growth, but actually fun.

My absolute favorite aspect of this movie is how Peele played on my expectations. It was as if he crawled inside my brain, examined all the gears, and pulled the right levers at the right time.

And by doing *that*—playing on my experiences—he took me on a hell of a ride.

That made me think about not only what my experiences were but how did Peele know mine? He certainly didn't find a secret door into my head as in *Being John Malkovich*.

Gradually it dawned on me that Peele used general human experiences anyone could relate to in his specific story.

So yeah, Jordan Peele used tropes (including the superpower **amnesia** one) in *Get Out*.

Let's take a look at how he did it.

Trope Synopsis: Get Out

Tortured hero Chris Washington is a talented Black photographer (**profession**) living in Brooklyn. He's dating Rose, a (**across the tracks**, **opposites attract**) White woman, who is eager to introduce him to her **family** outside New York City on their upcoming weekend away (**road trip**). Chris is apprehensive (**forbidden love**, **politics**, **red herring**) but Rose reassures him that her family is not racist (**the con**, **secret**). Chris' **best friend** and TSA officer, (**profession**, **protector**) Rod, offers reassurance while he dog sits for Chris.

Rose's **billionaire** family lives on an estate far away from New York City, where they will be holding their annual weekend summer party (**ticking time bomb**). Her father, Dean, is a neurosurgeon (**profession**), her mother, Missy, is a hypnotist (**profession**) and her brother, **loner** Jeremy, all live on their estate (**forced**

proximity). Chris feels isolated (**fish out of water**) and puzzled by how awkward the family's two Black **domestic servants**, housekeeper Georgina and groundkeeper Walter, act around him (**secrets**). Rose's family assures him they aren't racist (**politics**), but Chris feels something strange is going on (**red herrings**, **suspects**).

One night when he's having trouble sleeping, Missy (**antagonist**, **boss**) offers to hypnotize (**the con**, **amnesia**) Chris to cure his smoking habit. Chris tells Missy that his mother died in a car accident when he was a child which causes him a lot of guilt (**orphan**, **scar**). The next day, he finds himself no longer craving cigarettes (**red herring**, **second chance**). He also finds a box of photos with Rose (**hidden identity**) and past Black boyfriends when she earlier denied dating other black men (**stalker**, **secret**).

At the party, Chris sees a friend, Logan, from his neighborhood. Now, Logan is married to a much older wealthy White woman (**age gap**, **opposites attract**) but he behaves abnormally subdued and doesn't seem to remember Chris (**hidden identity**, **amnesia**). Chris tries taking a picture of him (**MacGuffin**, **mistaken identity**) on the sly. However, his cell phone camera flash goes off, triggering Logan to behave violently and yell at Chris, "Get out!" (**red herring**, **secrets**). Dean tells Chris that Logan had a seizure (**the con**) as he is removed from the party (**secrets**). Chris calls Rod after sending Logan's picture, and Rod confirms Logan's identity (**fake relationship**). Now Chris is seriously concerned about what is going on (**quest**). But Rose drains the cell battery on Chris' cell phone (**stranded**).

Protagonist in peril, Chris is **kidnapped** by Rose's family (**antagonists**) because Missy (**stalker**) installed some other commands on him under hypnosis that aren't smoking related (**amnesia**, **red herring**). Chris wakes up strapped to a chair (**stranded**, **violence**) and learns about the true reason he's there (**fake relationship**, **secrets**).

The purpose of the party is an auction (**ticking time bomb**) to win Chris' body (**MacGuffin**, **victim**) which will be the recipient of a wealthy, White blind artist's brain (**hidden identity**, **secret heir**, **twins**) after undergoing a surgical procedure. Chris realizes that is what has happened to Logan (**red herring**, **scar**, **victim**).

After the procedure, Chris' consciousness (**victim**) will be under the new brain's (**antagonist**) command by going into a "sunken place" (**secrets**, **stranded**); he will be aware of what his body is doing but unable to control it. Dean prepares to operate on Chris (**violence**, **ticking time bomb**).

Missy hypnotizes Chris recalling him into the "sunken place" (**stranded**, **time travel**) on her command. However, Chris has stuffed his ears with chair batting from his confinement so that he (**protector**) won't be influenced by Missy's commands (**the con**, **second chance**).

Chris attacks Dean, Missy, and Jeremy (**antagonists, suspects**), fighting them off and killing them (**redemption, violence**). He runs outside, jumps in a car, and starts driving when he accidentally hits Georgina, the housemaid (**victim**). Chris (**tortured hero**) recalls his mother's similar car accident and his inability to save her (**scar**). He helps Georgina into his car (**mistaken identity, red herring**) and starts to drive when she (**antagonist**) attacks him (**victim**). He sees the scars on her head showing she had the brain procedure (**fake relationship, hidden identity**). The car crashes, killing her.

We learn that Rose's grandmother's brain is in housekeeper Georgina's body and Rose's grandfather's brain is in groundskeeper Walter's body (**family, hidden identities, red herrings, suspects, ugly ducklings, victims**).

Rose shows up at the car accident firing a rifle (**violence**) at Chris. She calls Walter "Grandpa" (**fake relationship**) and orders him (**antagonist, hidden identity**) to attack Chris (**violence**). While struggling, Chris flashes his cell phone camera briefly neutralizing Walter (**red herring**). Again, the cell phone flash allows the sunken place personality to resurface in the groundskeeper's body (**second chance**).

Walter shoots Rose (**red herring, revenge**) and then himself (**violence**). A police siren's wail grows louder. Rose smiles (**red herring**) knowing that she'll look like the victim (**mistaken identity**) with a gunshot wound. Her smile implies (**the con**) that in this situation the impending interaction with Chris as a Black man with the police won't go well for him (**mistaken identity**, **fake relationship**).

The siren vehicle arrives (**red herring**). It's Rod's work car, not the local police (**mistaken identity**). Chris jumps in **his best friend's** car (**reunion**) and they head back to NYC (**return to hometown**), leaving Rose behind.

Discussion: Get Out

Ok, that is a packed plot with a lot of tropes embedded. I wanted to share how tropes are not the enemy of a story. Instead, they are used as building blocks to create a unique but relatable story.

The relatable part is important. One of the ways we are drawn into a story is by familiar feelings.

At the beginning of *Get Out*, Chris is apprehensive about going to a new place and meeting new people. That anxiety is something we can all relate to even if not in the exact way Chris does. But the setup pulls the audience in with, "hmm, let's see how this is going to go."

Now before I start waxing on about the **amnesia trope**, let's look at that author fan favorite tool—Goal, Motivation, and Conflict (GMC).

In *The Trope Thesaurus*, I talk about how Goal, Motivation, and Conflict (GMC) are key to developing tropes from building blocks into our individual stories.

I absolutely believe that is true in all genres including, of course, horror.

Chris:
Goal: get back to NY
Motivation: safety
Conflict: his life is in jeopardy

Rose:
Goal: bring Chris to family home for procedure
Motivation: control him
Conflict: Chris discovers the plot

Missy (hypnotist):
Goal: control Chris
Motivation: make him cooperate with the procedure
Conflict: he resists her hypnosis

How does GMC in *Get Out* reflect relationships?

It's all about manipulation of Chris' memories.

Missy and Rose are working to control Chris both by physically isolating him and by getting control of his memories.

Chris is fighting to stay independent, but he has inadvertently given Missy a huge advantage in controlling him.

So, without **amnesia** being only a surprise whack over the head, it's a trope that we can use to mine deeper character development.

In *Get Out*, the main story question is what will happen to Chris?

That's a great set up.

But for our purposes, let's look at how the **amnesia trope** fuels the story **conflict**.

To do that, we need to ask more of the **amnesia trope** in *Get Out.*

1) Who knows what?

Chris doesn't know anything, he becomes suspicious, but he is the last to know what Rose's family has planned for him.

2) How did the amnesia happen? Whomp over the head? Something else?

In Chris's case, he hasn't completely lost his memories yet. Right now, he's just under Missy's hypnotic control. He's got a surgical procedure in his immediate future to suppress his identity.

3) How and when are the memories coming back? Are they completely gone or are partial pieces slipping through?

To get the best bang for your buck with the **amnesia trope**, the memories *have* to return. That's where the whole **conflict** is, reconciling the loss and regaining the memories for our character. Chris has two big problems: (1) the suppressed guilt of his mother's accidental death, and (2) the very real threat that his whole personality could be submerged under another identity occupying his body.

To maximize story **conflict**, the memories must return at the worst possible time. For Chris, during his getaway from Rose's family, he accidentally hits the housekeeper. She has reminded him of his mother now that he is back in a similar situation to his own mother's accident. He stops and helps her into the car which ends up putting him at more risk, but he does it anyway.

4) What's the purpose behind the amnesia in this story?

There's nothing arbitrary about the **amnesia trope** in *Get Out.* Its purpose is to place Chris in jeopardy—physically and mentally—by manipulating his relationships.

5) What are tropes that work well with the amnesia trope? Let's take a look at them in *Get Out*.

Antagonist

This is always a "Winner! Winner! Chicken dinner!" trope in **amnesia**. Someone is pulling the strings in the memories game. For Chris, those **antagonists** are Rose's immediate **family** and the blind art dealer who wants to control his body.

Fake Relationship

In order to not lose the suspense created by the lost memories, there needs to be some **fake relationships** in this trope. The more intense that **fake relationship**, the better the reveal. The main one for Chris was how his girlfriend was setting him up all along to steal his body. She worked to gain his trust which made discovering the plan even more unthinkable for him.

Forced Proximity

This trope is a must with the **amnesia trope** because at some point in the story, we need the pressure of the memory loss and being in the **antagonists'** presence. Without it, we lose valuable story tension. If Chris could leave Rose's family's estate anytime he wanted the story would lose momentum. Instead, we see Chris getting more and more constrained until he is secured to a chair.

HIDDEN IDENTITY

This trope is another key part of the reveal. It works great with **fake relationship** here too. Chris learns about Logan's experience as a **victim**. It's someone he knows so his terror is two-fold; his outrage at what happened to Logan and his own impending future. Also, Chris doesn't perceive the housekeeper and groundskeeper as threats in the same way he does Rose's **family** because they are Black. When he learns that they have been surgically altered to house Rose's grandparents, he has put his escape in jeopardy by then.

POLITICS

I've come to appreciate this trope's power in horror and **amnesia**. **Politics** can be a big grand trope with comments on race, power, and wealth. All that is in *Get Out,* but thankfully it's so intertwined with the character development, this isn't a preachy story. The **politics** of how Rose's **family** hunts their **victims** is powerful in showing how they take down Chris and how he fights back.

PROTAGONIST IN PERIL

Usually in horror, we talk about the **woman in peril trope** but in this case, the one in peril is Chris. With the

amnesia trope, the memory loss is just another aspect of this trope. In Chris, it's not just his physical safety but his whole identity is at risk for being imprisoned under someone else.

Protector

Chris has his protective instinct awakened by seeing Logan and by his concern for the housekeeper and groundskeeper. In both those cases, he tries to help them. The **protector** role with **amnesia** is interesting because it's a way to show Chris' heroic qualities. He's been praised for his photography skills and not as a man of action, until now.

Red Herring

So many great uses of this trope with **amnesia**. It's another must-have but the key is to use the **red herring** skillfully. How does Peele do that? By planting little signs of misdirection, such as Logan's seizure when Chris' flash goes off. It's a strange overreaction from Logan, especially paired with him looking stunned and shouting, "Get Out!" at Chris. But Rose's physician father explains it was a seizure. That's plausible so Chris believes it, though he finds it unsettling. Then there's Rose's lie about dating Black guys and Chris finding the box of pictures.

Reunion

This is an important trope to include at the end as there is some kind of resolve to the story after the reveal. We always want to bring the story full circle after the main character has been on a **life-altering journey**. For example, Chris escapes back to the safety of New York City with his **best friend** picking him up in his TSA car. This echoes back to the first scene where his **best friend** argues he's a public safety officer and that statement is met with disbelief by Chris and Rose.

Scar

Please give your characters **scars**. Why? Because we, the audience, have them. Every one of us has had an experience that we can't shake. It informs our present day in a million little ways and occasionally big ones. Let's not deny the complexity of our characters! Chris' guilt over losing his mother in an accident as a child and not being able to do more is a great **scar**. It's specific and relatable. I haven't had this exact experience, but I feel his agony having had loss of my own.

Secrets

So many **secrets** here. If you're using the **amnesia trope**, your story needs lots of **secrets** for the **red herrings** and **reveals**. In *Get Out*, the **secrets** are everywhere because nothing is as it seems, especially regarding relationships.

Fake relationships and **hidden identity tropes** work so well with **secrets** and **amnesia tropes**.

Ticking Time Bomb (TTB)

If you've ever had a fleeting desire to be an event planner, a **TTB** gives you the opportunity to enact that fantasy. And even if you haven't, still use this trope in **amnesia**. The **TTB** is the external pressure to the reveal and it's often a public event. Why? Because even if we authors are a bunch of introverts happiest typing away in a dark hole, our character needs to experience a public event for maximum **conflict**. For Chris, he first experiences the **TTB** by attending Rose's family weekend visit. But then he realizes the impending surgical procedure is what he has to escape.

Time Travel

Like my new-found appreciation for the **politics trope**, I think of the **time travel trope** as a flashback is underrated. It's a way to use information about memories in our stories. For Chris, his **scar** about his mother is also a **time travel trope**. When he sees the injured housekeeper, he's emotionally transported back to a defining event of his childhood.

Ugly Duckling

A **transformation trope** like **ugly duckling** is always a good time in storytelling, but it's key to using the

amnesia trope. The **amnesia** experience has to change the character. For Chris, he initially thinks the hypnosis was a good idea because he no longer desires to smoke (also a great **red herring** by the way). The entire experience of that weekend at Rose's house has **transformed** him by the time Rod picks him up. He has escaped, killed in self-defense, and faced a past **scar**.

As we can see, the deep development of these tropes created a very unique story. And a different way to look at memories by showing us what happens when the relationships are manipulated. This is just such great storytelling material. Let's take a look at another example where dread about memories looms large.

Example #2

Severance (2022) Apple TV

What's more terrifying than ghosts or demons? A horror story set in a workplace.

The **monster** who's your coworker or **boss**.

Or worse yet—yourself.

For someone who spends a great deal of my waking hours thinking, studying, and talking about story structure—I didn't realize until well into my first viewing of *Severance's* first season, that the base of the story was the **amnesia trope**.

It's painful to admit, but there it is.

I didn't need to hear **amnesia** and start salivating for the story. What I heard was choosing to cut off memories...

This original take on the **amnesia trope** had me hooked from the set up. I am the *Severance* target audience; I'm always searching for ways to use the **amnesia trope** besides the convenient knock on the head. I find it fascinating that neither in the story nor in my extensive online obsessive reading about the series do I even run across the word **amnesia**. Instead, the focus is about access to painful memories.

Sounds similar to *Get Out* right?

Trope Synopsis: Severance

Widower, tortured hero Mark Scout is overwhelmed with grief from his wife's death (**scar**), elects to be severed—a surgical procedure that permanently separates his memories (**amnesia**) into two categories—his work life versus his private life (**twins**). A severed person's memory **transitions** during the elevator ride to/from the severed floor (**road trip**). Mark's "Outtie" (life outside his work) is as a **loner** despite his sister's (**family**) attempts to encourage him to socialize.

Meanwhile, Mark's work self or (his "Innie" identity) has no recollection of his life outside of work (**fish out of water, victims, stranded**) and no past memories (**amnesia**). He works (**profession**) at the **secretive** Lumen Corporation's (**fairy tale**) Macrodata Refinement Processing Department (MRP) (**forced proximity**) with three other employees (**victims**) and their supervisors, Mr. Melchek and Ms. Cobel (**antagonist, boss**).

As the story opens, Mark is promoted (**boss**) because MRP colleague #4, Petey (**best friend, boss**) has suddenly left Lumen Corp. Mark, Irving, and Dylan try to help their new replacement #4 colleague, Helly, settle into their division. However, she arrives freshly severed and fighting her procedure (**fish out of water**), finding her memory loss intolerable (**amnesia**). As her boss, Mark tries to **protect** her against running afoul of the Lumen rules with poor results. Helly's **hidden identity/across the tracks/billionaire/secret heir** tropes as the Lumen Company CEO's daughter are massive end-of-season reveals but little clues are planted along the way that she's not a regular employee. Later, Helly's "Innie" learns that her "Outtie" has chosen severance to further her **family's** business and **political** goals.

Mark's two non-severed **bosses**, Mr. Milchek and Ms. Cobel, struggle to keep Mark S.' increasingly unfocused division on meeting their quarterly goals (**ticking time bomb**). The team must capture and bin sets of numbers (**bet wager**) to clean the files before the quarter's end, but they don't know (**secret**) what the numbers refer to or represent (**MacGuffin**). The workers are kept in line by "visiting the breakroom," a confined space where they (**victims**) must repeat the same phrase hundreds of times (**time travel**) and receive physical punishment (**violence**).

Mark's severed floor **best friend**, Petey (who is on the run from Lumen), **stalks** him outside of work much to Mark's confusion. He has no memory of Petey outside of work because of severance. Petey explains who he is and what he's investigating—namely the **secretive** work of the MRP division (**MacGuffin**) and the nature of reversing the severed procedure. He asks Mark for his help before he dies (**bet/wager**) because he **suspects** Lumen Corp is the **antagonist**.

As the story progresses, Mark's "Outtie" (**protagonist in peril**) begins to investigate the clues Petey has left behind (**quest**). The clues lead Mark to witness the Lumen Security Chief's death by the surgeon who completes all the severance procedures (**boss**, **secret**, **violence**).

Meanwhile, back at Lumen, the team visits another department, Operations & Development (O&D), at the urging of the department head, Burt. He develops a friendship (**forbidden love**) with Irving in Mark's division.

Information sharing is formally discouraged between Lumen departments and treated harshly by the dreaded breakroom visits. Lumen's founder Kier Egan developed a strict set of principles for the employees to follow (**guardian**). There are rules and punishments for every small infraction along with a significant mistrust between departments (**fairy tale**).

Meanwhile, down on the severed floor in MDR things are changing (**forced proximity**, **workplace**). Helly tries to commit suicide (**violence**) to escape being severed but she is unsuccessful. Melchek and Cobel struggle to get Mark's department back under Lumen control and fail despite using the breakroom (**violence**).

Team member Irving has the most startling **journey** from handbook quoting sycophant to rejecting Keir Egan's rules to search for the newly-retired Burt. Team member Dylan, who is the reigning champ of MDR quotas, treats his severance with ambivalence. But when a stolen piece of Lumen property comes to Milchek's attention, the **boss** has no choice but to utilize the "overtime contingency" (**secret**, **fake relationship**, **hidden identity**)—bringing Dylan's "Innie" identity to the surface in his "Outtie" home setting. In the process, Dylan has a brief interaction with his young son (**family**) before Milchek revokes his "Innie" identity after he has retrieved the information.

The result is Dylan's "Innie" now has a scrap of a memory of his "Outtie" life (**secret**). This information tortures him so much that he attacks Melchek (**violence**). And he shares the overtime contingency information with his three colleagues (**secret**) so that they hatch a plan to wake their "Innie" identities in their "Outtie" bodies one evening (**hidden identities**).

Despite increasingly desperate attempts to keep Mark's division under control, the Macrodata Refinement Division (**ugly duckling**) is determined to break out of their "Innie" Severed floor prison while appearing to follow company protocols (**red herrings**, **fake relationship**).

Mark's unaware that his sympathetic next-door neighbor, Mrs. Selvig, is also his mercurial Lumen **boss**, Ms. Cobel (**hidden identity**). She is spying on (**stalking**) him to track the effects of his severance procedure and his grief (**secrets**). Mrs. Selvig also befriends Mark's sister as a nanny (**domestic servant, fake relationship, hidden identity**) to gain more information about Mark.

Like any large organization, the Lumen Corporation is full of **politics**. The tension between Ms. Coble, Natalie (the board's mouthpiece), and the mysterious board continues to increase over the season. When we learn Helly's "Outtie" identity and it makes much more sense why the **politics** pressure spikes.

The **blackmail trope** is used several times with Dylan telling Melchek that he'll tell Cobel about his interrupted sleep visit. Also, when Ms. Cobel tells Helly R. that if she goes onstage and tells the truth about being severed, she will inflict pain on her other team members at the season finale.

Every day after Mark and the other MRP members take the elevator away from the severed floor, they return to their "Outtie" lives (**return to hometown**).

Working together, the team activates their "Innie" identities during their "Outtie" evening (**mistaken identity, redemption**) trying to get their questions answered. Helly realizes her identity as Lumon's **heir**, and she prepares to speak to a crowd of **political billionaire** investors about her "Innie" experience when everyone else believes she is still her "Outtie" self; Helly hopes to tank Lumen Corp (**revenge**).

Mark's dead wife Gemma and Ms. Casey, the wellness resource director at Lumen, are one in the same (**amnesia**, **hidden identity**, **reunion**). Mark's wife did not die in a car accident (**red herring**, **fake relationship**) as he thought; she's been **kidnapped** by Lumen. Larger questions await such as the kiss between "Innie" Helly and "Innie" Mark.

In the final scenes, their "Innie" identities are woken up (**ugly duckling**, **quest/journey**) in their "Outtie" bodies (**fish out of water**, **amnesia**) at critical moments. Helly R. is about to tell the Lumen executives the truth about the severance procedure onstage at a fundraiser. Mark is at a party with his sister's family and Mrs. Cobel/Ms. Selvig is there when Mark sees a picture of his deceased wife and recognizes her as the human relations expert, Ms. Casey, at Lumen. Irving is knocking at the door of Burt's home as Melchek finally bursts in the room and dislodges Dylan from employing the overtime contingency. What happens next? I'm dying to know!

Discussion: Severance

Conflict is the character's self inflicted problem

Ok, let's look at how Goal, Motivation, and Conflict (GMC) work in developing the characters in *Severance.*

When we know what our characters really want, we can work out best how to torture them by putting conflict in their way.

Mark
"Innie"
Goal: discover his outside life
Motivation: freedom
Conflict: as an "Innie", he only exists at work. Trying to escape can mean death.

"Outtie"
Goal: find out what he's doing at Lumen during his work time.
Motivation: concern over his severance choice
Conflict: he has no access to his work-life memories.

Helly
"Innie"
Goal: leave Lumen
Motivation: freedom; she is caged at Lumen
Conflict: her "Outtie" self won't release her

"Outtie"
Goal: become severed
Motivation: benefit Lumen, her family's company
Conflict: her "Innie" tries increasingly violent ways to escape the severed floor, including attempting suicide

Mrs. Selivg/Harmony Cobel
Outside work
Goal: spy on Mark over his grief at his wife's death
Motivation: curiosity about the effectiveness of the severance procedure
Conflict: she's trying to not alert the Lumen Board of Directors that she has unrest on the severed floor at Lumen

At Lumen
Goal: make sure Mark's division meets their quarterly quota
Motivation: her own job depends on it
Conflict: Mark's team is increasingly hard to manage

But for our purposes how does the **amnesia trope** fuel the story **conflict**? WHAT IF YOU CAN'T IDENTIFY THE MONSTER just like Mark misses Mrs. Solveig/boss spying on him. The best monsters (in storytelling) don't need to have fangs. Hard to defend from the inside...

In *Severance*, the concept of missing memories is key to the whole story. Without the **amnesia trope** this wouldn't be the same story. The story focus is on what the effect is of painful memories on a variety of characters.

Severance also makes us think about the identity of the monster in this world. Is it the nosy neighbor? Is it the main character?

1) WHO KNOWS WHAT?

In *Severance*, the severed characters have two identities, one who retains all their memories and one who does not. It's an unequal relationship which causes increasing problems as the story develops. It's a pretty great concept to have characters keeping information from themselves. But it's more than just the severed individuals involved; their Lumen employers know much more about details of their employees' lives, which they are willing to manipulate.

2) WHAT HAPPENED?

The severed individuals chose to undergo elective (supposedly) permanent surgical procedures creating essentially two selves—their "Innie" (work-only selves only exist within Lumen building has no memories of outside life) and their "Outtie" (memory intact selves except about when they are at work which is not known to them). Mark chose memory loss which is a pretty interesting story idea, and we get to see the effects of his choice play out.

3) Are the memories coming back? When? How? Are they completely gone or partial pieces slipping through?

It turns out the severance procedure isn't irreversible, but the impact of the reversal operation is fatal as we see with Petey. Irving has problems with threatening images of a mysterious black goo swallowing up his life while working at Lumen. We're not sure what this means until the last episode when we see Irving painting the same image every night—the tunnel to the breakroom.

4) What's the purpose behind the amnesia if it was caused by someone/something?

The purpose for the memory loss depends on who we're talking about in *Severance*. For the "Outties" who chose severance, they have painful memories which they can't get relief from otherwise. But for the "Innies" whose whole identity is working in a windowless basement office, memory loss is a prison. And for the Lumen executives, severance is an opportunity to create a powerless workforce.

5) What other tropes work with the amnesia trope here? Let's take a look.

Antagonist

It's often said in fiction that the **antagonist** is the hero of their own story. *Severance* is a great example of that because Melichek, Ms. Cobel, or Hellie's "Outties" don't think they're bad people. They have reasons for their choices and often they are as mundane as meeting the quarterly quotas for their job or winning favor within a family.

Even Mark Scout's "Outtie" when questioned about his choice to undergo the severance procedure says, "I'm not a bad person."

Needless to say, the **antagonist** is a very powerful trope to use with **amnesia** because there's always someone interested in the protagonist not regaining their lost memories.

Fake Relationship

It makes sense that the **fake relationship trope** would be popular with **amnesia** because without it the character is missing crucial information about their relationships. Mark Scout is no different. He believes his wife died in a tragic auto accident. It's only in the last moments of the story that we see him make that connection between Ms. Casey at work and his wife in a picture.

Similarly, any relationships entered into on the Severed floor means none of the characters know who or what their lives are like outside work. Which is of course what makes Helly R. and Mark S.' kiss at the elevator so intriguing going forward.

The relationship between MDR rule follower Irving and Burt in O&D show the pair bonding over their love of art. Their friendship develops and deepens in a place where there is no allowance for identity because the severed workers have lost theirs. When Burt is suddenly retired, he and Irving know they will never see each other again. Burt's whole being will disappear because he doesn't exist as he is outside of Lumen. It's a wonderfully painful twist of the **fake relationship** and **forbidden love trope** that the relationship they share is true yet unsupportable.

FORCED PROXIMITY

The framework of the severance idea is based on the **forced proximity trope**. In their work location, the employees have one set of experiences but when they leave Lumen, they aren't able to access them. It's the perfect setup for employer abuse (aka the breakroom and the security system which screens any note passing) because there's no way to seek outside intervention.

Plus, **forced proximity** means the employees must interact often increasing the likelihood of **conflict**. It's a workplace as a prison. I also like that the "Outties" are experiencing a dreary Northeastern winter because it keeps the characters inside and reacting to each other.

HIDDEN IDENTITY

To keep tension tight, it's necessary to not only use **forced proximity** but double up with character identities when using the **amnesia trope**. Why? Because when there is a reveal, such as Mark's niece's party, the **hidden identities** collide. In his Outtie world, Mrs. Solveig is his nosy but carrying next-door neighbor. But down on Lumen's severed floor, the same woman is his **violent** and demeaning **boss**, Ms. Cobel. That discovery at the party, paired with his missing niece triggers a deliciously tense **red herring**. Has Ms. Cobel taken Mark's niece? After a frantic search it is revealed that she did not but it's a great diversion at a tense time.

MACGUFFIN

The **MacGuffin** is a powerful trope in driving most plots and paired with **amnesia** that's no exception. But what's interesting about how the **MacGuffin** is used in *Severance* is that instead of searching for a tangible thing, which is its usual application, the **MacGuffin** is lost memories. Mark and the rest of the MRG team all want to know what they are missing but there's no way to learn that from inside the Severed floor. Instead of all competing for the **MacGuffin** as an individual object, the team bands together to break out and find their missing memories.

POLITICS

Workplace group dynamics at MRP is thrown into turmoil when the former group leader, Petey, unexpectedly resigns. His replacement, Helly, is newly severed and she fights being severed. Her nonconformity causes upheaval in the normally sedate MRP division.

Another political relationship that is complicated with **amnesia** is Helly's "Innie" struggle with her "Outtie" self who agrees to severance as a means of gaining **family** approval. It's a great way to use the **twin trope**, **politics**, and **amnesia**.

PROTAGONIST IN PERIL

Mark S. and the rest of his MRP team are in danger from the Lumen Corp. as soon as they start wanting to know more about what severance has removed from their lives.

Outside of Lumen, his former coworker and best friend, Petey, contacts him, convincing him to investigate the company. Mark attends Petey's funeral and he learns from the surgeon who did the procedure that it may be reversible. He has to conceal his connections with Petey from anyone who might work at Lumen.

In Mark's case, we learn that his missing memories are being tested by his **boss**, Ms. Cobel, by her having Human Resources' Ms. Casey repeatedly meet with him. Ms. Casey is his wife and neither of them realize that. If he were to though, it seems given Ms. Casey will be sent away to a research lab, and Mark could wind up there too.

Red Herrings

This trope and **amnesia** work together in teasing reveals.

Early on Mark S. covers for Helly's rebelliousness and gets sent to the break room as punishment. He returns bruised but as he's leaving the Lumen parking lot that evening, he finds a gift certificate on his windshield. It explains he had an accident at work and provides a free dinner for him. It's a **red herring** because we think, oh he's going to have to explain the injury. But no, he goes along with the explanation and free dinner. His sister implies that he gets many free dinners for being clumsy at work and the whole thing is suspicious.

In the final episode, when Mark's niece goes missing at the party and we see Ms. Cobel/Mrs. Selvig speeding away in her car, we assume that she has taken the baby with her. She knows Mark's "Innie" is conscious outside of Lumen. She is racing to Lumen to warn everyone. But the frantic search for his missing niece provides misdirection. When we know she is safe with her parents we are relieved and curious about what Ms. Cobel is going to do at Lumen next.

SCAR

The **scar** in *Severance* is the motivation for the procedure. In Mark's case, we know he lost his wife. As for Dylan, Irving, and Helly R, we have no more idea than they do what their life outside Lumen is like.

This story does a great job of showing that removing the memories doesn't stop them from wondering. Since they don't remember making the severance procedure decision, they have had their "Outtie's" choice imposed on them. The loss of choice for the "Innies" is worse than the painful memories, at least for them.

SECRETS

Any engaging **amnesia** story is packed with **secrets** and *Severance* is no exception. What is interesting about this story is that Mark's "Outtie" friends and **family** are aware of his double life. When he's asked at a dinner party about his work on the severed floor, Mark has nothing to tell them because he has no memory of the work there.

Gradually though, with Petey's help, the secrecy about what the MRP department does begins to gnaw at both "Innie" and "Outtie" Mark. He, along with Helly, Irving, and Dylan end up wanting to know what they are really doing cleaning "scary" numbers.

Ticking Time Bomb (TTB)

Having a time-sensitive limit works great to increase **conflict** with the **amnesia trope**. In Severance, the **TTB** is that they all need to meet the department's quarterly goal by the due date. Even though Mark, Irving, and Dylan are competent at processing data, it's a new experience for Helly. And one that isn't easy to understand. She does get the hang of cleaning the scary numbers but it's down to the wire for her to complete the task.

There's more than just team spirit at risk here; their entire plan to **secretly** access their "Innie" personas after leaving Lumen, requires a distraction. That comes in the form of the end-of-quarter reward for the best refiner—Dylan. And he selects the coveted waffle party, which he uses to sneak away from and access the security office. Each of these events is dependent on the others and has a narrow time slot. The **ticking time bomb** works so well with **amnesia** to set up the reveal. After Dylan is successful, he has to hold off Melchik from breaking into the security office to stop him. That's another **ticking time bomb**. What's better than one **TTB**? Two or more.

Ugly Duckling

The **transformation trope** of **ugly duckling** works with **amnesia** because manipulating memories is a risky business. Of course, there are going to be complications and revelations. If it was easy as wiping memories to create a docile workforce, the Lumen Corp wouldn't need Ms. Coble and Mr. Melchik to control the employees.

When MRP star programmer Dylan steals a game card from Burt's O&D division, Melchik has no choice but to activate The Overtime Contingency. This is where Melchik wakes up Dylan's "Innie" in his "Outtie" body at home.

Dylan is stunned by this development as well as to find himself in a closet with Melchik. While his **boss** presses him for where the card is that he stole, Dylan looks around at his life which seems pretty normal until his school-aged son breaks into the closet to hug him. Dylan tells Melchik where to find the card, but he has many questions about his life at Lumen.

At the end of the series, we are left gasping about how this story will continue. It's been renewed for a second season so it will be really interesting to see how the **amnesia trope** is continued. In the meantime, I console myself with rewatching it on a semi regular basis catching new little clues each time. I love that about a great story, but it can be so intimidating to us as creators.

Amnesia Further Reading

If you're looking for books to read as excellent **amnesia** examples (and I really hope you are!) start with these three: Daniel O'Malley's *The Rook,* David Wong's *John Dies at the End* and Jeff Vandermeer's *Annihilation.*

Conclusion

Right now, I hope you are becoming mildly obsessive about tropes. Or at the very least bathed in tropes. My hope is that all this discussion makes them less intimidating or awkward to work with. They are just a tool in your writer's bag of tricks that you use for building your story.

Embrace the dread that we can create in our characters. It will keep your audience riveted for what will happen next in your story. Look for tropes in your own stories and those you consume by books or movies. Study how they are introduced and built upon.

Thank you for reading Horror Trope Thesaurus! Will you consider leaving an Amazon review (or other point of purchase review?), I'd really appreciate it. Thanks again, Jen

Sign up for my newsletter here (https://dl.bookfunnel.com/tvbb2jpx9x) and receive my **6 Steps for Story Structure** pdf free.

Check out what I'm up to at: www.jenniferhilt.com

Goal = The object of desire

Motivation = the "why" do we want this? (the goal)

Conflict = what comes from encountering obstacles

Antagonist = the force creating obstacles to the goal

Protagonist = the one who, ~~distov~~ in searching for goal, discovers truth.

Index

Part One

* There are a million diff ways to imagine or label the protagonist's role, but this one truly is so universally true and instantly adds so much depth.

Part Two

Part Three

Acknowledgments

Thank you to my family and friends for indulging my horror binge fest this summer. I also appreciate the feedback from Amy, Dana, Steven, and Victor after reading earlier drafts. Thanks to Charity Chimni and Cool, Calm and Corrected for all their help making this manuscript shine. And thanks to Bookin' It Designs for my cover.

About the Author

I'm a USA Today Bestselling author who has worked as a plotter and concept creator. I've written 24 books across four pen names. I have degrees in linguistics and literature. I live in Seattle with my family and my canine fan club. I love collecting dictionaries in unfamiliar languages, bingeing Scandi-Noir streaming series, and shouting out tropes from the comfort of my couch.

For my non-fiction titles sign up for my non-fiction newsletter (https://dl.bookfunnel.com/tvbb2jpx9x). For my fiction titles visit https://www.jenniferhilt.com to sign up for my fiction newsletter. Stop by and see what else I'm up to!

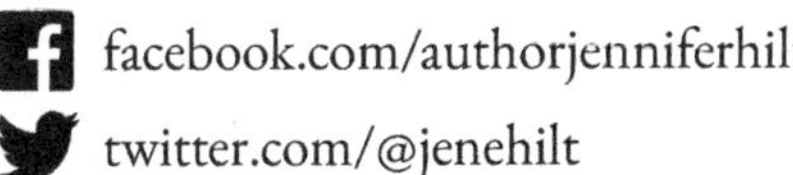

facebook.com/authorjenniferhilt

twitter.com/@jenehilt

instagram.com/jennifer_hilt

bookbub.com/authors/jennifer-hilt

Also by the Author

URBAN FANTASY

The Undead Detective

The Undead Detective Bites

The Undead Detective Hunts

The Undead Detective Slays

NON-FICTION

The Trope Thesaurus

Horror Trope Thesaurus

Romance Trope Thesaurus

Made in the USA
Middletown, DE
03 November 2022